GOD
SPEAKS YOUR
LOVE
LANGUAGE

GOD
SPEAKS YOUR
LOVE
LANGUAGE

HOW TO FEEL AND REFLECT GOD'S LOVE

GARY CHAPMAN

NORTHFIELD PUBLISHING

CHICAGO

Editor of revised edition: Stan Campbell
Cover Design: Studio Gearbox
Cover Image: Dougal Waters/Digital Vision
Author Photo: Boyce Shore & Associates

Library of Congress Cataloging-in-Publication Data

Chapman, Gary, 1938-
   God Speaks Your Love Language / Gary Chapman.
      p. cm.
   Includes bibliographical references.
   ISBN 978-0-8024-7275-5
   1. Love—Religious aspects—Christianity. I. Title.

BV4639 .C425 2002
241'.4—dc21
2002071862

This book is printed on acid free recycled paper containing 30% PCW (Post Consumer Waste) and manufactured in the United States of America by Bethany Press.

We hope you enjoy this book from Northfield Publishing. Our goal is to provide high-quality, thought-provoking books and products that connect truth to your real needs and challenges. For more information on other books and products written and produced from a biblical perspective, go to www.moody-publishers.com or write to:

Northfield Publishing
820 N. LaSalle Boulevard
Chicago, IL 60610

1 3 5 7 9 10 8 6 4 2

Printed in the United States of America

To my sister,
Sandra Lane Benfield,
who loved God as intensely as anyone I have ever known,
and expressed it by serving others.
Though younger than I, she beat me to the finish line.
I pray that my love will be as transparent as hers.

CONTENTS

ACKNOWLEDGMENTS

This book could not have been written in the isolation of an ivory tower. Wherever the love of God is experienced, it is always personal, intimate, and life changing. I am indebted to the scores of people who allowed me into the inner chambers of their own encounters with God.

Without such private information, the book would have been an academic treatise. For the most part, I have used fictitious names, but the people are real, and their stories an accurate account of what they told me. To all of them, I am deeply grateful.

For technical help, I have relied again upon Tricia Kube, my secretary and administrative assistant for the past twenty-five years. Thanks to Stan Campbell for his editorial input on this "freshened" message. The editorial, production, and marketing staffs of Northfield are not only my colleagues, but my friends. My gratitude for them runs deep.

My wife, Karolyn, has for forty years been my chief cheerleader. I have often felt God's love through her words of encouragement. In the midst of writing this book, we experienced the death of my sister, my only sibling, to whom this book is dedicated, and twelve hours later, the birth of our first grandson. Through the emotions that accompany death and birth, she walked with me. Two are truly better than one.

To my sister's family—husband Reid and daughters Traci, Jill, and Allison—I can only pray that the love of God, which she experienced and freely gave, will spill over on you and me, and that we may be as faithful as she.

THE LOVE
CONNECTION

Susan was my first appointment of the day, and I felt like crying when I heard her story. Her father had committed suicide when she was thirteen. Her brother was killed in Vietnam. Six months ago, her husband had left her for another woman. She and her two small children were living with her mother. I felt like crying . . . but Susan wasn't crying. In fact, she was vibrant, almost radiant.

Assuming she was in denial of her grief, I said, "You must feel very rejected by your husband."

"I did at first, but I've come to realize that my husband is not running from me. He is running from himself. He is a very unhappy man. I think he believed that our marriage would make him happy, but you and I both know that only God can make a person truly happy."

Thinking that perhaps Susan was trying to spiritualize her pain, I said, "You have been through a lot in your life: your father's death, your brother's death, your husband's departure. How can you be so strong in your faith?"

"For one reason," she said. "I know that God loves me, so no matter what, He is always there for me."

"How can you be so sure?" I asked.

"It's a personal thing. Every morning, I give the day to God and ask Him to lead me. I read a chapter in the Bible and listen to what He says to me. God and I are very close. That's the only way I can make it."

Later the same day I had an appointment with Regina. Her parents had divorced when she was ten years old. She saw her father only twice after the divorce: once at her high school graduation and again at her younger sister's funeral. Her sister had been killed in an auto accident at the age of twenty-one. Regina had been married and divorced three times; the longest of her marriages had lasted two and one-half years. She was in my office because she was contemplating a fourth marriage. Her mother had asked that she talk with me before she married again.

"I don't know if I should do this or not," Regina said. "I don't want to grow old alone, but I don't have a very good track record with marriage. I feel like I am a loser. My mother keeps telling me that God loves me and has a plan for my life. Right now I don't feel God's love, and I think I must have missed the plan. I'm not even sure there is a God."

Two ladies, each having experienced enough pain for a lifetime. One feels deeply loved by God; the other feels empty. Why do some people claim to experience God's love very deeply, while others feel so distant from God that they are unsure God even exists? I believe the answer lies in the nature of love itself. Love is not a solo experience. Love requires both a lover and a responder. If God is the divine lover, why do not all of His creatures feel His love? Perhaps because some are looking in the wrong direction.

Most often, one's search for God is influenced by culture. If our culture says, "This is the way to God," then we tend to pursue according-ly. But love is a matter of the heart, the soul—not ritual or religion. I am convinced that each of us has a "primary love language," and when we listen to God in our "heart language," we will experience His love most intimately. I am also convinced that God speaks each person's love language fluently. Perhaps this is best understood by examining how love works in human relationships.

HEARING THE LANGUAGE OF LOVE

In other volumes, I have dealt with the problem of not hearing love in our own language. My clinical research has revealed that a variety of love languages exist. Thus, if parents don't speak a child's primary love language, the child will not feel loved, regardless of how sincere the parents may be. The key is learning the primary love language of each child and speaking it regularly. The same principle is true in mar-riage. If a husband doesn't speak his wife's love language, she won't feel loved—and her need for love will go unfulfilled.

The Five Love Languages (which has now been translated into close to fifty languages) focuses on helping couples learn how to effectively communicate love. Later, I teamed up with psychiatrist Ross Campbell and wrote *The Five Love Languages of Children.* This book helps parents learn how to love their children effectively. Next came *The Five Love Languages of Teenagers,* which is designed to help parents navigate the turbulent waters of loving their children through the adolescent years. Most recently I wrote *The Five Love Languages for Singles* which helps singles understand and experience love in all of their relationships.

For individuals who have a genuine desire to grow closer to the people they love, these books can provide the knowledge needed to do so. But there are a significant number of people for whom knowl-edge is not enough. (Actually, all of us fall into this category from time to time. We know what to do, but don't have the will to do it.) One husband, having heard my ideas on learning to speak a spouse's primary love language, said, "I'll tell you right now, if it's going to take my washing dishes, vacuuming floors, and doing laundry for her to feel loved, you can forget that." Obviously his problem was not a lack of knowledge; he simply lacked the will to love his wife.

The tragedy is that people who choose not to love are never happy people. Their lack of love hurts not only the other person, but it atrophies their own souls as well. People who refuse to love live on the edge of desperation.

I have spent a lifetime trying to help people who, to borrow a line from Oscar Hammerstein's "Ol' Man River," are "tired of living and scared of dying." The purpose of this book is to bring people closer to God so they can first feel His limitless love and then reflect it in order to more effectively love others. To love and to be loved—what could be more important?

I believe that the key to learning and choosing love is tapping into divine love. However, this is not intended to be a "religious" book. If a religious system were able to solve the problem of a loveless society, it would have already done so. This book is an attempt to help people relate to the God who is there, not the gods that culture has created. I have chosen not to write in the academic language of psychology or theology, but in the language of the layperson, so more people might hear God's words spoken in their "heart language."

If you believe in God and would like to be more loving toward those closest to you, then this book can help. If you don't believe in God, but are willing to consider the opinion of someone who does, I invite you on the journey. I will make every effort to respect your position while I share my own beliefs as clearly as I can.

CONNECTING TO A PARENT'S LOVE

If people are created in the image of God and are His children, we would expect Him to love us. Also, it would be natural to not only receive love, but also to reciprocate that love. This is illustrated in the parent-child relationship.

For most parents, loving children comes as naturally as eating does for the child. Parents love because they are related to their children. In a very real sense, the child is a creation of the parents and bears in his or her body and spirit something of each parent's mark. It would be extremely unnatural for parents not to love their own children. It is widely agreed upon that parental love is a part of human nature. It is not something we work to attain. It is a part of who we are as human beings.

A parent's love for his or her own children (and a grandparent's love for his or her own grandchildren) is more intense than the love felt for the child next door (or the grandchild who belongs to a best friend). But this love is not simply a genetic bonding, for adoptive parents and grandparents love their children just as intensely. There is an emotional and spiritual bonding with those children whom we consider "ours." We are willing to expend time, energy, and money to promote their well-being. We want them to learn and develop their potential. We desire that they accomplish great things in life. We are willing to give much of ourselves in order to enhance their lives. We love them. This is the normal emotional response of parents toward children and grandparents toward grandchildren.

The naturalness of parental love is highlighted by the statistical contrast of the few parents and grandparents who do *not* feel such love for children and grandchildren. The absence of parental love is so abnormal that those parents are considered dysfunctional and in need of psychological and spiritual therapy. Loving one's children is as natural as loving oneself, for indeed, children are extensions of the parents.

REFLECTING DIVINE LOVE

I believe that parental love is a reflection of divine love. In God's eyes, we are His children, and He loves us as we love our own children. *World Book Encyclopedia* describes God as "the supreme being, the creator and ruler of the universe, all knowing, all powerful, infinite, and ever present."[1] Throughout history and across racial and cultural boundaries, millions of people have believed in the existence of such a God. The ancient Hebrew writings began with the assumption of an all-powerful God who created the heavens and the earth. Then, in an orderly fashion, He created plant and animal life and culminated His creation by making human beings in the image of the divine.[2]

If it is true that people are made in the image of God, then we would expect God's love for humankind to be in a category different from God's love for the rest of His creation. We would also expect that people would be capable of responding to God's love. What research has revealed is that not only do people have the potential for responding to the love of God but, in fact, they are not fully content until they have made a loving connection with God.

Victor Frankl, who survived Nazi imprisonment in four concentration camps, including stays in Bohemia and at Auschwitz, reminded us that at the heart of everyone's existence is the search for meaning. Saint Augustine wrote that people never truly find ultimate meaning until they respond to the love of God.

Brian, a friend of mine, was touring Russia after the collapse of communism. He noticed that on Sunday the churches were filled with people. Knowing that for seventy years Russia had been an atheistic society and that a whole generation had been taught that God does not exist, he was intrigued to notice that so many young people were attending church. He asked his young female guide, a former member of the KGB, if people had flocked to the churches immediately when given the freedom to do so.

"No," she said. "At first, it was only the older people. Then the young people began to attend. Now all the churches are filled."

"Why do you think that is true?" Brian inquired.

"Earlier," she said, "we believed that our political leaders were gods. Now we know that is not the case. We have learned that man is man and God is God. Now we wish to know more of God."

If people are truly made in the image of God, this response is what we would expect. In spite of all governmental efforts to stamp out the belief in God, the human heart still craves the Father's love.

This father-hunger is reflected in human relationships. In his book *Life Without Father,* David Popenoe, a sociology professor at Rutgers University, gives compelling evidence that all children crave the love not only of a mother but also of a father. Something within the souls of children knows that they need a father's love to be secure and happy. When that love is not experienced, a child lives with an indefinable longing. Children want to love and be loved by both parents. Popenoe believes that the lack of this love connection is the major malignancy we face in our time.

People need to reestablish the "love connection" with God, their heavenly Father. (I will refer to this term, as well as making the "God connection," throughout this book.) To know and to love God should be our chief end; all else is simply background music.

What I hope to do in this book is to share what I have learned about love during more than forty years of marriage and family counseling. I believe that human love relationships reflect the nature of God, who is love. If we can understand the dynamics of human love, it will help us better comprehend the expressions of divine love.

In doing so, I want to introduce you to friends I have met along my own journey. (In most instances, only first names are used [and changed], and details have been altered to protect privacy.) Some are people I have known for many years; others are more recent acquaintances. But all of them have made the love connection with God. I have been helped and inspired by their stories, and I hope you will be too.

At the end of each chapter, you will find a few questions to help you apply the lessons others have learned to your own life. In addition, there is a guide for group study in the back of the book. It can be very helpful to consider and discuss the content in a group setting. And even if you don't have the opportunity to do so, you may find some additional insight by perusing that material on your own.

Chapter One

UNDERSTANDING *the* FIVE LOVE LANGUAGES

After more than forty years of counseling couples and families, I am convinced that there are five basic languages of love. There may be many "dialects," but only five languages.

Each person has a primary love language, which means that one of the five love languages speaks more deeply than the other four on an emotional level. When someone speaks my primary love language, I am drawn to that person because he or she is meeting my basic need to feel loved. When a person does not speak my primary language, I will wonder whether he or she really loves me because emotionally I do not connect as strongly with that person.

The problem in many human relationships is that one person speaks a particular love language and wonders why another person with a different love language does not understand. That's like my speaking English to someone who understands only German and wondering why he doesn't respond. Human relationships are greatly improved when basic language barriers are removed—and are even more enhanced when we learn to speak each other's love language.

TRANSFORMING MARRIAGES

Thousands of married couples echo the story of Scott and Anna. They had driven four hundred miles to Atlanta to attend a "Love Languages" seminar. After the Friday night session, Scott said, "Dr. Chapman, we want to thank you for turning our marriage around."

I was confused because they had just started the weekend seminar. Sensing the question in my eyes, Scott continued. "God used *the love language concept* to transform our marriage. We have been married for thirty-three years, but the last twenty years have been utterly miserable. We have lived in the same house and been outwardly friendly with each other, but that's as far as it went. We had not taken a vacation together in twenty years. We simply didn't like being with each other.

"Some time ago, I shared my misery with a friend. He gave me your book and told me to read it. I went home and finished reading it at about two o'clock in the morning. I shook my head and asked myself, *How could I have missed this?*

"I realized immediately that my wife and I had not spoken each other's love language for years. I gave the book to her and asked her to read it. Three or four days later, we sat down and discussed it. We both agreed that if we had read the book twenty years earlier, our lives would have been different. I asked her if she thought it would make any difference if we tried now. She replied, 'We don't have anything to lose.'"

At this point, Anna broke into the conversation and said, "I didn't have any idea that things would actually change between us, but I was certainly willing to give it a try. I still can't believe what has happened. We enjoy being with each other now. Two months ago, we actually took a vacation together and had a wonderful time."

As the conversation continued, I learned that Scott's primary love language was words of affirmation and Anna's was gifts. (All five love languages will be summarized later in this chapter.) Scott was not a gift-giver by nature. In fact, gifts meant very little to him. He got no special thrill when he received a gift, and he had little interest in giving gifts. Conversely, Anna was a woman of few words. She was not given to compliments and admitted that she was often critical.

It was not without effort that Scott learned to buy gifts. In fact, he recruited his sister to help him with the project. Anna admitted that at first she thought it would be a temporary phenomenon. Their original agreement was that for three months they would speak each other's love language at least once a week and see what happened.

"Within two months," Scott said, "I had warm feelings for Anna and she had feelings for me." Anna said, "I never dreamed that I would be able to say the words 'I love you' to Scott and really mean it. But I do; it's incredible how much I love him."

When a husband and wife discover each other's primary love language and choose to speak it on a regular basis, emotional love will be reborn.

TRANSFORMING SINGLE RELATIONSHIPS

Single adults have also benefited greatly from understanding the five love languages. As one example, let me share with you a letter Megan sent me from Japan.

Dear Dr. Chapman,

I wanted to let you know how much your book, *The Five Love Languages,* has meant to me. I know you wrote it for married couples, but a friend gave it to me and it has had a profound impact on my life.

I am in Japan teaching English as a second language. The main reason I came here was to get away from my mother. Our relationship has been strained for several years. I felt unloved and that she was trying to control my life. When I read your book, my eyes were opened. I realized that my love language is words of affirmation, but my mother only spoke to me with critical, harsh words.

I also realized that my mother's language is acts of service. She was forever doing something for me. Even after I got my own apartment, she wanted to come over and vacuum my floors. She knitted a sweater for my dachshund and baked cookies when she knew I was having friends over. Since I didn't feel loved by her, I saw all of her efforts as attempts to control my life. Now I realize it was her way of expressing love to me. She was speaking her love language and I know now that she was sincere.

I mailed a copy of the book to her. She read it, and we discussed it via email. I apologized for misreading her actions over the years. And after I explained to her how deeply her critical words had hurt me, she apologized to me. Now her emails are filled with words of affirmation. And I find myself thinking about things I can do for her when I get home. I have already told her that I want to paint the bedroom for her. She can't do it herself and can't afford to have it done.

I know that our relationship is going to be different. I have helped some students here learn to speak English a little better, but my greatest discovery has been the languages of love.

TRANSFORMING CHILDREN

Parents also must learn the primary love languages of their individual children if the children are to feel loved. Marta was the mother of five-year-old Brent when she had her second child. About two months after the baby arrived, she began to notice a change in Brent who until then had been what she called "a perfect child."

She said, "We never had any trouble with Brent. But almost overnight we began to notice behaviors that we had not seen before. He would do things that he knew were against the rules and then deny that he had done them. We noticed that he was deliberately rough in handling the baby; once I found him pulling the blanket over the baby's head in the crib. He began to defy me. I remember the time he said, 'No, and you can't make me!'"

Marta began attending a ladies' group that was studying *The Five Love Languages of Children.* She said, "When I read the chapter on quality time, I knew what was going on with Brent. I had never thought of it before, but I realized that quality time was Brent's primary love language. Before the baby came, I spoke his language loudly and he felt loved. Afterward, we no longer took walks in the park together, and our quality time was greatly diminished. With this insight, I went home determined to make time for Brent. Rather than doing housework while the baby slept, I began to spend time with him.

"It was amazing to see the results. Within four or five days, Brent was back to being the happy child he had always been. I couldn't believe how quickly he had changed."

The craving for love is our deepest emotional need from childhood onward. If we feel loved by the significant people in our lives, the world looks bright and we are free to develop our interests and make a positive contribution in the world. But if we do not feel loved by the significant people in our lives, then the world begins to look dark and the perceived darkness will be reflected in our behavior.

TRANSFORMING TEENAGERS

In the heart of the teenager, love has to do with *connection, acceptance,* and *nurture.* Connection requires the physical presence of the

parent and meaningful communication. Acceptance implies unconditional love regardless of the behavior of the teen. Nurture is feeding the
spirit of the teen with encouragement and comfort. The opposite of
connection is abandonment. The opposite of acceptance is rejection.
And the opposite of nurture is abuse—physical or verbal.

Any teenager who feels abandoned, rejected, or abused will almost
certainly struggle with self-worth, meaning, and purpose. Eventually
the pain of feeling unloved will show up in the destructive behavior of
the teenager.

Yet negative behavior often changes radically and quickly when the
teenager genuinely feels loved by parents. Speaking a teen's love language can transform the parents' relationships with him or her.

THE FIVE LOVE LANGUAGES

The five love languages are more fully explained in my previous
books, but let me briefly review them here.

(1) Words of Affirmation

Using words to affirm another person is one key way to express love.
Affirmations may focus on the person's behavior, physical appearance,
or personality. The words may be spoken, written, or even sung. People whose primary love language is words of affirmation receive such
affirming words like a spring rain on barren soil.

There are thousands of ways to express verbal affirmation. Here are
just a few examples:
- "You look nice in that dress."
- "You did a good job with that assignment."
- "I appreciate your sticking with this project until you finished."
- "Thanks for cleaning your room."
- "I appreciate your taking out the garbage."

- "This was a great meal."
- "Thanks for all your hard work."

(2) Quality Time

Quality time is giving someone your undivided attention. With a small child, it may be sitting on the floor rolling a ball back and forth. With a spouse, it is sitting on the couch, looking at each other and talking . . . or taking a walk down the road, just the two of you . . . or going out to eat and engaging in good conversation. With a teenager it is going fishing and telling him what your life was like at his age, then asking how his life differs from yours. (You focus on the teen—not the fishing.)

For the single adult, quality time is planning an event with a friend where the two of you have time to share your lives with each other. The important thing is not the activity, but the time spent together. When you give someone quality time, you are giving him or her a part of your life. It is a deep communication of love.

(3) Gifts

Giving gifts is a universal expression of love because gifts are the product of loving thoughts. Children, adults, and teenagers all appreciate gifts. But for some people, gifts are a primary love language. To them, nothing compares with a gift for making them feel more loved.

Gifts need not be expensive. You can pick up an unusual stone while hiking, give it to a ten-year-old boy, tell him where you found it, and let him know you were thinking of him. I can almost guarantee you that when he is twenty-three he will still have the stone in his dresser drawer.

(4) Acts of Service

"Actions speak louder than words." The old saying is especially true

---

for people whose primary love language is acts of service. Doing something that you know another person would like to have done is an expression of love. Examples include cooking a meal, washing dishes, vacuuming floors, mowing grass, cleaning the grill, giving the dog a bath, painting a bedroom, washing the car, driving the sixth grader to soccer practice, mending a doll dress, and putting the chain back on a bicycle. The list could be endless. The person who speaks this language is always looking for things he or she can do for others.

To the person whose primary love language is acts of service, words may indeed be empty if they are not accompanied by action. A husband can say, "I love you," but the wife thinks, *If he loved me, he would do something around here.* He may be sincere in his words of affirmation, but he is not connecting emotionally because her language is acts of service. Without seeing him act, she does not feel loved.

A wife may give her husband gifts, but if his love language is acts of service, he wonders, *Why doesn't she spend her time cleaning the house instead of buying me things?*

"The way to a man's heart is through his stomach" does not apply for all men, but may well be true for the man whose primary love language is acts of service.

(5) Physical Touch

The emotional power of physical touch was known to mothers for centuries before science proved it to be true. That's why we pick up babies, cuddle them, and say all those silly words. Long before the child understands the meaning of love, he or she feels loved by physical touch.

If the child's primary love language is physical touch, nothing is more important. Hugging and kissing a six-year-old as he or she leaves for school in the morning is the best preparation for a day of learning. Teenagers whose primary love language is physical touch may begin to draw back from your hugs and kisses, but it does not mean that they have lost the desire for touch. They associate hugs and kisses with childhood. Since they are not children any longer, you must learn new "dialects," new ways of touching them—a slap on the shoulder, an elbow at an appropriate moment, high fives after noteworthy achievements, a back rub after a tough dance practice, etc. But if you stop touching those teenagers, they will feel unloved.

WHAT LOVE LANGUAGE DOES GOD SPEAK?

Another concept I have explained in other books is that of a person's "love tank." Think in terms of a gasoline gauge on a car. Right after a fill-up, you can drive for long periods with little concern about fuel. But if you ignore the need for too long, you're likely to find yourself stranded and in need of help.

Similarly, any person's "love tank" needs to be replenished on a regular basis. The key to making sure that your spouse, children, and parents feel loved is to discover the primary love language of each person and speak it consistently. If you speak someone's primary love language, his or her love tank will remain full and the person will be secure in your love. Then you can sprinkle in the other four love languages as "icing on the cake." However, if you don't speak a person's *primary* love language, he or she will not feel loved even though you may be speaking some of the other languages. The person's love tank gauge remains on empty.

This book builds on the concepts from my previous books and considers the love languages of God. It is my premise that the love languages observed in human relationships all reflect various aspects of divine love. If people are indeed made in the image of God, and if people have five distinct love languages, then we would expect to find all those love languages expressed in the character and nature of God. Indeed, God speaks *every* language, so it is not surprising to discover that He communicates fluently through each of the five love languages. However, people tend to be most responsive to God when they detect that He is speaking their primary love language.

In the pages that follow, you will observe the perspectives of numerous contemporary and historical individuals who established a love relationship with God. As you examine the nature of those relationships, you can learn how to enhance your own love connection with God.

QUESTIONS FOR REFLECTION / DISCUSSION

(1) If the concept of the five love languages is new to you, which of the five options do you think is your *primary* love language? Why? (You may not be sure at this point, but future chapters will provide much more information for you.)

(2) If you are familiar with the five love languages, can you think of a time when "speaking the wrong language" created problems between you and another person? If so, how do you think a similar problem could develop in your relationship with God?

(3) What initial questions do you have that you hope this book will help you answer?

Chapter Two

GOD SPEAKS LOVE LANGUAGE #1:

WORDS *of*
AFFIRMATION

I fondly recall the conversation that started a thought process that eventually resulted in this book. I would like to share the story with you.

I had flown into Chicago and then had been driven two hours to reach an inner-city church. I arrived late and took a seat near the back where I tried to be inconspicuous. The music was over and the sermon had begun. The pastor was waxing eloquent, and his multicultural congregation was giving him plenty of encouragement.

"That's right, Brother Reuben. Preach it!" I heard one elderly gentleman shout.

"Thank You, Jesus," a lady to my right said with her eyes closed and her right hand lifted high.

My driver, whom I had met at the airport, had filled me in on the history of the church and its leader. "When Pastor Reuben came here," he said, "we only had about thirty members. Now we have two thousand.

The church was dead, but he loved us. He knows how to motivate people, and God has blessed."

My host told me about the church's ministry to the homeless—how they had turned a nearby warehouse into a shelter that now housed more than 150 people every night. He told me about their soup kitchen. "I go down three days a week and help serve lunch," he said. "It's the highlight of my week." He told me about their recovery program for young people who were addicted to drugs.

I was thinking about all he had told me as I sat in the back of the church and listened to Pastor Reuben, who wove words together in a fascinating way. I still remember the three points of his sermon: (1) God knows you; (2) God loves you; and (3) God wants you. I listened as he walked through the Old and New Testaments, giving illustrations for each of his points. He talked about the Hebrew prophets as though they were his friends. He quoted from Scripture freely.

"Listen to the words of God to ancient Israel," he said: "'I have loved you with an everlasting love; therefore I have drawn you with lovingkindness.'[1] Do you think that God loved Israel more than He loves you? And listen to these words about Jesus as He faced death: 'Jesus knowing that His hour had come that He would depart out of this world to the Father, having loved His own who were in the world, He loved them to the end.'[2] God has always loved His children; God will always love His children; and He wants you to be His child," Reuben said with deep passion.

I was tired and sleepy. The building was hot. But I never once nodded as I listened to this master wordsmith make his case for the love of God, calling his listeners to repentance and faith in Christ. As he gave his plea for sinners to come to Christ, several people left their seats, walked to the front, and bowed at the altar. Many were weeping. "Come home, come home," Reuben pleaded. "God loves you too and wants you to be His child."

Eventually the service neared an end and Reuben called me to the front. He introduced me to the congregation because I had been invited to speak the next night at a marriage enrichment event for the couples of the church. Then, after the service, Reuben's wife, Patsy, invited me to their house for dessert and to meet the couple who directed their marriage enrichment ministry.

After we got acquainted and were beginning to relax, I said to Patsy, "Describe your husband to me. What kind of man is he?" (Being a marriage counselor, I can get away with those kinds of questions.)

"Oh, he is definitely a romantic," she said. "He writes me poems; sometimes he sings songs to me. He gives me speeches about how wonderful I am."

"Then you must have a full love tank," I said.

"That's the problem. I've read your book, and my love language is acts of service. I want him to wash the dishes," she said, laughing. "You know, vacuum the floor, take out the garbage, help me around the house. I know he loves me, but sometimes I don't feel loved. His words sometimes seem empty. It's almost like he's trying to humor me. I know he's sincere, but I need more than words."

I sensed that this conversation had gone a little deeper than I had intended, so I told Patsy, "You sound like my wife. Her love language is also acts of service. It took me a long time to get the connection between washing dishes and love." I laughed and changed the subject. Reuben was also laughing, and in less than a minute we were talking about the Chicago Bears.

The next night after the marriage enrichment session was over, Reuben drove me to my hotel after dropping Patsy off at their house. As we drove away from the house, Reuben said, "You have stimulated my thinking. I've got a good wife. We've been married for seventeen years, but I'm not sure that I'm meeting her emotional needs. This love language concept has opened my eyes. I'm definitely going to read your book. I think I've got some homework to do."

I was impressed by Reuben's sensitivity and openness. I reemphasized how long it had taken me to discover the love language of my wife, and I shared what a difference it had made in my own marriage.

About a year later, I met Reuben again at a national pastors' conference in Chicago. He ran up to me, gave me a big bear hug, and said, "I just want to tell you what a difference you made in my marriage and in my ministry. I have been using your five love languages in my counseling and teaching ever since you came to our church. And Patsy told me that if I saw you to tell you that I am now washing the dishes." We both had a good laugh, and I asked him if we could spend some time together that afternoon. I wanted to converse with this man who had made such a strong impact on so many lives.

Among other things that afternoon, I asked Reuben to tell me about his conversion to Christ. "Well, it's a long story," he began. "When I was a young boy, my mother took me to church. The pastor was an older man who preached often about the love of God and how God valued the individual. I remember he said, 'God will love you when everyone else walks away from you. Everybody is somebody in God's eyes.' He motivated me to want to be somebody.

"My mother always wanted me to go to college, so I worked hard in high school so I could attend. Unfortunately, when I got there, I associated with the wrong crowd. Before long I was partying more than I was studying. One night near the end of my freshman year, I was at a party and had too much to drink. The next morning I woke up lying in a field nearby and had no idea how I'd gotten there. I sat up, wiped my eyes, and heard the birds singing. And as clear as a bell, I heard the words of my old pastor: 'God will love you when everyone else walks away from you. Everybody is somebody in God's eyes.'

"I started weeping. I knew those words were true, and I knew I was walking in the wrong direction. I wept for a long time, and then I said to God: 'Forgive me for acting like a nobody when in Your eyes, I'm somebody. Forgive me for walking away from Your love. If You will forgive me and come into my life, I will be somebody for You.'

"It was like the scales fell off my eyes," Reuben continued. "I felt like I had come home from a long journey. I knew that God had forgiven me, and I knew that He wanted me to tell others about His love. I was saved and called to preach while sitting in that field that morning.

"That weekend I went home and told my mother what had happened. She shouted all over the house, praising God that He had saved her boy. She called the pastor and told him what had happened, and he invited me to tell the people at church. So the next Sunday I gave a testimony of what God had done in my life and told the congregation that I intended to follow Him and be a preacher.

"I've been walking with Him ever since. I changed my college major to speech with a minor in English, and I preached every time I got an opportunity. When I got to seminary, a little church called me to be their pastor. So I pastored while I attended seminary."

"Do you enjoy preaching?" I asked.

"I'd rather preach than eat, and you know how preachers like to eat," Reuben said with a smile on his face. "When I'm preaching, I feel like I'm doing what I was created to do. It's my way of saying thank You to God for what He's done for me. I feel closest to God when I'm preaching."

THE AFFIRMING WORDS OF GOD

What Reuben shared with me that afternoon stimulated the research that has led to this book. It was clear that Reuben's primary love language was words of affirmation. He spoke them freely to his wife, and I later learned that his encouraging words characterized his relationships with others. In his marriage, he had not always felt loved by Patsy because she often used critical words about his not helping her around the house. But after they identified each other's primary love language, Patsy started giving him verbal affirmation, and he began to speak her love language—acts of service. As a result, the emotional climate of their marriage greatly improved.

The thing that struck me from Reuben's story is that the way people interrelate on a human level tends to be true on a spiritual level as well. Reuben responded best to words of affirmation, and that's how God got through to him as a wandering college freshman. Reuben remembered the words of his pastor: "God will love you when everyone else walks away from you. Everybody is somebody in God's eyes." To him, they were words from God that moved him deeply. And once he had come home to God, his first desire was to express his love to God—again, through words of affirmation. He would affirm the love of God to others through the power of the spoken word.

Some people—even pastors—find public speaking very difficult. But Reuben felt closest to God when preaching. It was his way of saying thank You to God.

Reuben taught his congregation the other love languages as well. He taught that giving gifts to God (tithes, offerings, our time and skills in service) is one expression of love, and that people show love to God by serving others. He acknowledged the discipline of meditation and prayer in which one spends quality time with God, as well as the value of touching others. But for Reuben, the most natural expression of *his* love to God was in using words both to affirm God and to encourage others.

Was Reuben's experience with God unique? Not at all. The Bible is filled with illustrations of God speaking words of affirmation. In fact, the Bible itself is often known as the "Word of God." The phrase, "The word of the Lord came to [Isaiah, Jeremiah, etc.]," is found frequently throughout the Old Testament prophetic books to affirm that the message was from God rather than the prophet.

The New Testament further explains: "All Scripture is God-breathed and is useful for teaching, rebuking, correcting and training in righteousness, so that the man of God may be thoroughly equipped for every good work." It also says, "You must understand that no prophecy of Scripture came about by the prophet's own interpretation. For prophecy never had its origin in the will of man, but men spoke from God as they were carried along by the Holy Spirit."[3]

All of the words from God affirm the worth of human beings. Modern nihilistic thinking concludes that people are worthless and their lives have no meaning, but that is not the message of the Scriptures.

In the first chapter of the Bible we read, "Then God said, 'Let us make man in our image, in our likeness, and let them rule over the fish of the sea and the birds of the air, over the livestock, over all the earth, and over all the creatures that move along the ground.' So God created man in his own image, in the image of God he created him; male and female he created them."[4] Whatever else this passage means, it places people above the animals and gives them the capacity to have a relationship with God.

The New Testament affirms the creation account. The writer of Hebrews wrote (quoting the psalmist) that God made people a little lower than the angels and has crowned them with glory and honor.[5]

All of the specific commands of God in both the Old and New Testaments affirm our worth, flow from His love, and direct us toward a higher goal. Some people find the commands of God restrictive and rebel against them. But those who know God believe that His prohibitions are designed to keep them from those things that would destroy them. They also believe the admonitions of God are designed to help them experience life's highest good.

God's people accept the words of the prophet Isaiah, "This is what the LORD says—your Redeemer, the Holy One of Israel: 'I am the LORD your God, who teaches you what is best for you, who directs you in the way you should go. If only you had paid attention to my commands, your peace would have been like a river, your righteousness like the waves of the sea.'"[6]

The God of the Bible is characterized as the God who speaks. His words are designed to build a relationship with people. The Scriptures consistently declare God's words of encouragement:

- *"Do not fear, for I am with You; do not be dismayed, for I am your God. I will strengthen you and help you; I will uphold you with my righteous right hand."*
- *"For I know the plans I have for you . . . plans to prosper you and not to harm you, plans to give you hope and a future."*
- *"I have loved you with an everlasting love; I have drawn you with loving-kindness."*
- *"I will turn their mourning into gladness; I will give them comfort and joy instead of sorrow."* [7]

THE AFFIRMING WORDS OF JESUS

The words of Jesus of Nazareth confirmed those of God in the Old Testament Scriptures. They bring life and hope to all people who respond:

- *"I tell you the truth, whoever hears my word and believes him who sent me has eternal life and will not be condemned; he has crossed over from death to life."*

- *"I am the bread of life. He who comes to me will never go hungry, and he who believes in me will never be thirsty."*
- *"For my Father's will is that everyone who looks to the Son and believes in him shall have eternal life, and I will raise him up at the last day."*
- *"My sheep listen to my voice; I know them, and they follow me. I give them eternal life, and they shall never perish; no one can snatch them out of my hand. My Father, who has given them to me, is greater than all; no one can snatch them out of my Father's hand. I and the Father are one."*
- *"'Behold, I am coming soon! My reward is with me, and I will give to everyone according to what he has done. I am the Alpha and Omega, the First and the Last, the Beginning and the End. . . .' Whoever is thirsty, let him come; and whoever wishes, let him take the free gift of the water of life."* [8]

Jesus came to demonstrate the love of God, giving Himself as a sacrifice for the misdeeds of every man and woman. Jesus said He was God's Son. Who can fathom the depths of the love of Jesus, who, while being crucified, prayed, "Father, forgive them, for they do not know what they are doing"? [9] The words of Jesus clearly affirmed His love for humanity. His love was unconditional.

He stated His purpose clearly when He said, "I am the gate; whoever enters through me shall be saved. . . . The thief comes only to steal and kill and destroy; I have come that they may have life, and have it to the full. I am the good shepherd. The good shepherd lays down his life for his sheep." [10]

From beginning to end, the Bible pictures a loving God who declares His love by speaking words of truth, comfort, and redemption. Such words of affirmation are a love language that God speaks fluently.

RESPONDING WITH WORDS OF AFFIRMATION:
MARTIN LUTHER

Many individuals testify that a "God connection" resulted from reading the Bible. One example is Martin Luther. As a young monk, Luther sought to find peace with God by living a life of strictest asceticism. Sitting alone in his room, deeply concerned about his relationship with God, Luther opened his Bible and began to read Paul's letter to the Romans. When he came to Romans chapter 1, verse 17, he read, "The just shall live by faith" (KJV). He paused. He pondered. Then joy unspeakable flooded his heart.

He had tried hard to please God by a life of discipline. Now his eyes were opened—he understood salvation was by faith, not works. This word from God was to him the "gate to Paradise." From that moment, Martin Luther's life focused on listening to the words of God. For him, the Bible was the Word of God. His newfound devotion inspired him to stand against the established church of his day, which placed more emphasis on tradition and religious efforts than on the Scriptures. His desire was that people would return to the Word of God.

Martin Luther's primary love language seems to have been words of affirmation, based on accounts of his life and his personal letters. In correspondence to his beautiful wife, Katharine, he began, "To my dearly beloved wife Katharine Luther, for her own hands. God greet thee in Christ, my dearly loved Katie! I hope . . . that I can come [home] tomorrow, or the day after. Pray God that he bring me home safe and sound." To Hans, his six-year-old son, he wrote, "Grace and peace in Christ, my dear little son. I hear with great pleasure that you are learning your lessons so well and praying so diligently. Continue to do so, my son, and cease not."[11]

In the realm of the spiritual, Martin Luther used powerful words in numerous ways to express his devotion to God. His words were both convicting and affirming as he wrote hymns and Bible commentaries, developed a catechism, translated the Bible from Latin to German, and delivered thousands of sermons. While other monks meditated, Luther was speaking and writing.

His best-known hymn, "A Mighty Fortress Is Our God," focuses on the power of the Word of God. Take a look at Luther's words in verse 3:

And tho' this world, with devils filled,
Should threaten to undo us,
We will not fear, for God hath willed
His truth to triumph thru us:
The prince of darkness grim,
We tremble not for him;
His rage we can endure,
For lo, his doom is sure,
One little word shall fell him.

Luther is also remembered for his ninety-five theses, carefully thought out, written down, and nailed to the door of the castle church in Wittenberg, Germany. Luther's list of fundamental beliefs would light the fires of the Reformation.

RESPONDING WITH WORDS OF AFFIRMATION: KING DAVID

Perhaps the best biblical example of a person whose primary love language was words of affirmation is David, the second king of Israel. On many occasions, David indicated how deeply he was moved by the words of God. Here are just a few examples:

- " How sweet are your words to my taste, sweeter than honey to my mouth! I gain understanding from your precepts; therefore, I hate every wrong path. Your word is a lamp to my feet and a light for my path."

- "Your statutes are my heritage forever; they are the joy of my heart."

- "I have put my hope in your word."

- "I rejoice in your promise like one who finds great spoil. I hate and abhor falsehood but I love your law. Seven times a day I praise you for your righteous laws. Great peace have they who love your law, and nothing can make them stumble."[12]

David also used words of affirmation in response to God, as an expression of his love:

- *"May those who love your salvation always say, 'The LORD be exalted!'"*

- *"I will praise God's name in song and glorify him with thanksgiving. This will please the LORD more than an ox, more than a bull with its horns and hoofs."*

- *"Oh, how I love your law! I meditate on it all day long. Your commands make me wiser than my enemies."*

- *"My mouth will speak in praise of the LORD. Let every creature praise his holy name for ever and ever."*

- *"Praise the LORD. Praise the LORD, O my soul. I will praise the LORD all my life; I will sing praise to my God as long as I live."*[13]

Clearly David's primary method of expressing his love to God was through words of praise, thanksgiving, and adoration. If you have any question about David's primary love language, read Psalm 18, in which David responds after God has delivered him from his enemies. For fifty verses, he expresses his love to God in some of the most beautiful language ever written.

David had access to only the five books of the Hebrew Bible (typically referred to as the Pentateuch or the Torah), but clearly, he saw them as the words of God. He said of the Scriptures, "Your word, O LORD, is eternal; it stands firm in the heavens. . . . Your laws endure to this day, for all things serve you. If your law had not been my delight, I would have perished in my affliction. I will never forget your precepts, for by them you have preserved my life."[14]

David saw all of God's words—laws, ordinances, commandments, precepts, testimonies, statutes, and judgments—as being expressions of who God is. He took them as ultimate truth, as certain as God Himself. He based his life on the words of God. As best we can determine, David wrote seventy-three of the Psalms found in the Bible. Many of them are expressions of praise and thanksgiving to God. His words are some of the most heartfelt emotional literature in the Bible. David clearly expressed his devotion to God through words of affirmation.

"MY PRAYERS FLOW WITH PRAISE"

One way God expresses His love is through words, and many people respond to Him primarily through words of affirmation. This was certainly true for my pastor friend Reuben, for Martin Luther, and for King David.

This was also true of Jason, whom I met in Riverside, California. He told me, "My love language is words of affirmation. Once my wife started speaking affirming words, my love for her grew more intense."

Much later in our conversation, I asked him, "When do you feel closest to God?"

Jason responded, "I feel closest to God when I am singing praise to Him and when I am praying. My prayers flow with praise and thanksgiving to God, telling Him how much I love Him."

Thousands of contemporary followers of Jesus can identify with Jason. Their hearts have been captured by the words of God, and they reciprocate His love by expressing words of praise. But many others would have a different answer to my question than the one Jason gave.

For another significant group, their method of worshiping and expressing their love to God does not focus on words, but on quality time. We will turn our attention to that group next as we examine another love language of God.

QUESTIONS FOR REFLECTION / DISCUSSION

(1) How have you ever been touched by someone else's words of affirmation toward you? Think of some examples.

(2) When was the last time you used words of affirmation to encourage another person? How consistent were you? What was the result?

(3) How does God use words of affirmation to encourage you?

(4) How might words of affirmation be incorporated into your worship of God? (Songs? Scripture reading? Poetry? Prayer? Serving as liturgist?)

Chapter Three

GOD SPEAKS LOVE LANGUAGE #2:

QUALITY TIME

Greta was a fellow speaker at a national women's conference in Los Angeles. After I had finished my lecture describing the five love languages and the importance of understanding and speaking another person's primary love language, she rushed over to me and said excitedly, "We have got to talk." I didn't know what she wanted to talk about but, after hearing her lecture on women and spirituality and observing her exuberant spirit, I was certain the conversation would not be boring. We agreed to meet the next afternoon.

When we got together, Greta dived right into the subject. "Let me tell you my thoughts from last night. After hearing your lecture, it struck me that God speaks to us in our primary love language, which explains why some people have dramatic, emotionally moving conversions.

"For example," she continued, "my husband was converted at a church that a work colleague had invited him to visit. The second

Sunday he attended, the friend asked if he would like to go to the front and have people pray for him. Not wanting to offend his colleague, he agreed. Several men gathered around him and began to pray aloud at the same time. My husband said that he had never heard anything like it. But within five minutes, he was weeping uncontrollably and asking God to forgive him. He said the sensation was like electricity running through his body, and he felt totally clean. It was like God actually touched him.

"When he came home and told me about the experience, I didn't want anything to do with it. To me it was religious emotionalism, and I couldn't believe that he had gotten caught up in it. But he continued to attend the church and began to bring home books for me to read.

"My own conversion was very different. It came through months of prayer, reading the Scriptures, and contemplation. I was motivated to keep searching because I knew how important my husband's spiritual experience had been to him. But I never had a dramatic experience like his. Rather, little by little, I began to realize that I was becoming a follower of Jesus. As I continued to read the Scriptures, it was like God began to speak to me. I realized that what I was reading was truth and that behind the truth was a God who loved me."

Nine months after her husband's conversion, Greta was having her normal Bible reading and meditation time one morning. She read Revelation 3:20, where Jesus said, "Here I am! I stand at the door and knock. If anyone hears my voice and opens the door, I will come in and eat with him, and he with me." As Greta put it, "It seemed so clear that for the past several months God had been knocking at the door of my life. That morning I actually said to Him, 'Come in. I want to share the rest of my life with You.'

"I didn't cry. I wasn't emotionally excited," Greta explained. "It was a quiet, calm moment during which my heart opened up and allowed

God to come into my life.

"Now I see it all so clearly. My husband's primary love language is physical touch, and my primary love language is quality time. God spoke both languages and led both of us to understand He loves us," Greta said. "I have never fully understood my husband's experience, and he wonders how I can be so calm about my relationship with God. But both of us know that we are followers of Jesus. It has had the most profound effect upon both of our lives."

Almost without taking a breath, Greta continued, "Last night I realized that not only does God speak our primary love language to show His love to us, but we speak our primary love language in showing our love to God. My husband expresses his love to God by singing praise songs in church. He will lift both hands toward God, often close his eyes, and sing with all his heart. I will sometimes see tears running from his eyes as he sings. His emotions are stirred. He often says, 'I felt the presence of God.' I would never do that," said Greta. "That's just not me."

"So how do you express your love to God?" I asked.

"By spending quality time with God, of course," she said. "You didn't need to ask me that; you already knew," she said with a smile. "My greatest joy is spending time with God in studying the Scriptures. I can spend a whole morning. I lose track of time. My husband finds it hard to spend more than ten minutes reading the Bible or a devotional book. He would much rather be in church singing praise songs and 'feeling the presence of God.' I realize now that he is as sincere as I. It's just that we speak different love languages to God."

I saw Greta two years later at a marriage conference. She introduced me to her husband, Rod. "This is the man who taught me how to love you," she told him. Rod had that bewildered look on his face until she said, "He wrote the book *The Five Love Languages.*"

Rod smiled and said, "Our marriage has changed. I couldn't believe it when Greta came home and started speaking my language. You will be pleased to know that we have a date night every week and every evening we have fifteen minutes of 'couple time.' I'm making sure that Greta's love tank is full."

When I inquired about how the love language concept had affected their worship of God, Rod said, "Oh, I still raise my hands in praise to God and Greta still spends her time meditating." They both laughed and Greta said, "It's true. But now we are giving each other freedom to express our love to God differently."

THE JEWISH PATRIARCHS AND ANCIENT ISRAEL

Biblical and postbiblical history confirms what Greta and Rod learned about experiencing the love of God. The Old Testament Scriptures describe how God spent quality time with Adam and Eve. In the cool of the evening, they walked and talked together in the Garden of Eden. It was only after the Fall that Adam and Eve hid themselves from God, knowing they had betrayed His trust in them.[1]

Later, Abraham was called the "friend of God." God often spoke personally with Abraham. On one occasion when God was about to bring judgment on the wicked city of Sodom, where Abraham's nephew lived, God said, "Shall I hide from Abraham what I am about to do?"[2] In fact, God did not withhold His intentions but actually engaged in a dialogue with Abraham, who sought to persuade Him not to destroy the righteous along with the wicked. God agreed to spare the city if as few as ten righteous people could be found living there. And when ten could not be found, God first delivered Abraham's nephew Lot and his family before passing judgment on Sodom.

The Psalms often speak of God's love for those He created and His desire to draw near and spend quality time with them. For example,

"The LORD is righteous in all his ways and loving toward all he has made. The LORD is near to all who call on him, to all who call on him in truth."[3]

Through the prophet Isaiah, God spoke of His love for Israel and promised His presence would be with them in times of trouble. "Fear not, for I have redeemed you; I have summoned you by name; you are mine. When you pass through the waters, I will be with you; and when you pass through the rivers, they will not sweep over you."[4]

The psalmist spoke of an intimate love relationship with God based on God's willingness to give him focused attention: "I love the LORD, for he heard my voice; he heard my cry for mercy. Because he turned his ear to me, I will call on him as long as I live."[5] The psalmist was drawn to God because of God's willingness to talk with him in his time of need.

The New Testament describes a similar relationship with God as James promises, "Come near to God and he will come near to you."[6]

THE LIFE AND MINISTRY OF JESUS

The idea that the eternal God desires to spend quality time with His creatures is one aspect of faith unique to Christianity. The gods who have been created by the imagination of human minds have always been far removed from people's daily life. The gods of the ancient Greek and Roman myths had to be placated or feared. The idea of having a close personal relationship with those deities did not exist.

On the other hand, Jesus indicated that the desire of the entire Trinity—God the Father, God the Son, and God the Holy Spirit—was to "abide" (make a home) with anyone who responds to God's love.[7] Jesus promised never to leave His followers, but told them that He would be with them forever. In one of Jesus' prayers, He said, "Father, I want those you have given me to be with me where I am, and to see my glory, the glory you have given me because you loved me before the creation of the world."[8] Clearly, Jesus desired quality time with all of those who responded to His love.

The design of Jesus' earthly ministry was an illustration of quality time. He preached to the multitudes, but He spent quality time with twelve individuals. "He appointed twelve . . . that they might be with him."[9] Later He would appoint those men as apostles to carry on His ministry. So in preparation, Jesus spent quality time with them to convince them of God's love for humankind.

Jesus did not attempt to make His ministry as *broad* as possible, but rather as *deep* as possible. He wanted His chosen apostles to experience His love at the deepest possible level. For three and one-half years they shared meals, travels, experiences, and extended conversations. He taught the multitudes in parables, but provided the Twelve with a much fuller explanation of His message during their special times together.

Of course, Jesus also spent quality time with other individuals. On one occasion, He and His disciples visited a woman by the name of Martha and her sister, Mary. After the formality of greetings, Martha busied herself in the kitchen preparing a meal for Jesus and His disciples while Mary sat enthralled with His teaching. Martha was disturbed that her sister was not helping her with the meal. She eventually became so agitated that she actually entered the room, interrupted Jesus, and asked Him if He would please instruct her sister to help her.

Jesus did not respond as Martha hoped. He acknowledged her acts of service, yet made it clear that He was also pleased with Mary's undivided attention. Jesus knew the heart of both sisters. Martha was concerned about doing the proper thing, but she was not motivated by love. In fact, her sense of duty had distracted her from developing a love relationship with Jesus.

My guess is that Martha's love language was acts of service and Mary's was quality time, both of which can be valid expressions of one's love to God. On this occasion, however, Martha's attention seemed based on ritual rather than relationship. She put performance above the person of Christ. She was doing what came naturally for her—acts of service—but her heart was not in it. In much the same way, those whose primary love language is words of affirmation can often speak empty religious words with no conscious love toward God. All authentic love for God flows from a heart that genuinely seeks to honor Him.

THE STORY OF GEORGE MUELLER

History is replete with individuals whose primary love language was quality time and who expressed their love to God by spending what to others would have been inordinate amounts of time in prayer, Scripture reading, meditation, and undistracted attention on God. George Mueller (sometimes spelled Müller) was one of those persons. Born in Germany in 1805, Mueller dedicated himself at age twenty entirely to the service of God. He was a theology student at the University at Halle and mastered six languages: Latin, Greek, Hebrew, German, French, and English.

From the beginning of his ministry, Mueller refused any salary for himself and would not solicit contributions for the ministries that he started. He believed that faith in God and reliance on prayer would provide all his needs. His ministry included free distribution of Bibles and other Christian literature, the establishing of Christian day schools for the poor, and, most notably, a commitment to orphanages. By 1875 his orphanages had lodged, fed, and educated over two thousand English children.

Mueller's purpose in running orphanages was twofold. In his own words:

I certainly did from my heart desire to be used by God to benefit the bodies of poor children bereaved of both parents, and seek in other respects with the help of God to do them good for this life. I also particularly longed to be used by God in getting the dear orphans trained up in the fear of God; but still, the first and primary object of the work was and still is that God might be magnified by the fact that the orphans under my care are provided with all they need, only by prayer and faith without anyone being asked by me or my fellow laborers, whereby it may be seen that God is faithful still, and hears prayer still.[10]

Even before Mueller started orphanages, his lifestyle was characterized by extended periods of quality time with God. The following are excerpts from his diary.

- July 18, 1832: "Today I spent all morning in the vestry, to procure a quiet season. This has been for some time the only way, on account of the multiplicity of engagements, to make sure of time for prayer, reading the word, and meditation."
- July 19, 1832: "I spent from half past nine till one in the vestry. Had real communion with the Lord. The Lord be praised, who has put it into my mind to use the vestry for a place of retirement!"
- June 25, 1834: "These last three days, I have had very little real communion with God, and have therefore been very weak spiritually, and have several times felt irritability of temper."
- June 26, 1834: "I was enabled, by the grace of God, to rise early, and I had nearly two hours in prayer before breakfast. I feel now this morning more comfortable."
- September 29, 1835: "Last evening when I retired from the family, I had a desire to go to rest at once, for I had prayed a short while before;

and feeling weak in body, the coldness of the night was a temptation to me to pray no further. However, the Lord did help me to fall upon my knees; and no sooner had I commenced to praying than he shone into my soul, and gave me such a spirit of prayer as I have not enjoyed in many weeks. He graciously once more revived his work in my heart. I enjoyed that nearness to God and fervency in prayer for more than an hour, for which my soul had been panting for many weeks past. . . . I went to bed especially happy, and awoke this morning in great peace, rose sooner than usual, and had again, for more than an hour, real communion with the Lord before breakfast. May he in mercy continue this state of heart to his most unworthy child."[11]

For George Mueller, quality time with God was the center of his life and enabled him to sense deeply the presence and peace of God. When he missed quality time, he felt a distance between God and himself. (He warned fellow believers that "often the work of the Lord itself may be a temptation to keep us from that communion with him which is so essential to the benefit of our own souls.")[12]

After being sick for three months and unable to minister, he wrote on January 14, 1838: "I have spent several hours in prayer today, and read on my knees, and prayed for two hours over Psalm 63. God has blessed my soul much today. My soul is now brought into that state that I delight myself in the will of God, as it regards my health."[13] Clearly Mueller's quality times with God were not ritualistic, but deep and personal. They affected the whole of his life.

On May 7, 1841, he wrote: "Now, I saw the most important thing I had to do was to give myself to reading the word of God, and to meditation on it; thus my heart might be comforted, encouraged, warned, reproved, instructed; and that thus, by means of the word of God, whilst meditating on it, my heart might be brought into experimental communion with the Lord."[14] It was this "experimental communion with the Lord" that enabled Mueller to perform his ministry.

Many who look back on the life of Mueller are inclined to praise him for his work with orphans and the establishment of schools for the poor of England. Contemporary Christians are impressed that he did so without the solicitation of funds that is so common to philanthropic endeavors in our generation. For Mueller, however, his ministry was simply the outgrowth of his quality time with God. Communion with God was far more important in his mind than caring for the poor. "This I most firmly believe," he once wrote, "that no one ought to expect to see much good resulting from his labors in word, and doctrine, if he is not much given to prayer and meditation."[15]

Although his life was characterized by acts of service and words of affirmation for the benefit of others, Mueller's primary love language was quality time. He spoke it fluently as he developed his love relationship with God.

Such extended times of communion with God have seemed incomprehensible to both contemporaries of Mueller and those who have read of his life and ministry in ensuing years. Some assume he was a "supersaint," driven to please God. Others have sought to explain Mueller's lifestyle by focusing on the culture in which he lived. Life was much simpler 175 years ago when people moved at a slower pace and had more time for meditation and contemplation.

While this is certainly true, Mueller was one of the busiest men of his generation. Imagine the time required to oversee orphanages in various locations and numerous schools for the poor children of the cities. Clearly Mueller would have had as many demands on his time as any modern-day administrator. A better explanation, it seems to me, is that Mueller experienced the love of God most deeply during his quality times. It was from that well that Mueller drew not only his vision, but his energy. In those times of contemplation as he focused on listening to the voice of God through Scripture, Mueller was energized to carry on the ministry to which he was called.

When someone's primary love language is quality time, uninterrupted times of communion with God are not difficult but joyous, not burden-causing but burden lifting. As Mueller said, "The first great and primary business to which I ought to attend every day is to have my soul happy in the Lord. The first thing to be concerned about is not how much I might serve the Lord, how I might glorify the Lord; but how I might get my soul into a happy state, and how my inner man might be nourished."[16]

SPEAKING IN A NATIVE TONGUE

For Mueller and thousands like him, quality time is a native tongue. It is the most natural way of experiencing the love of God and reciprocating.

Recently a woman told me, "I feel closest to God when I have my daily quiet time with Him. It is the most important part of my day. When I miss that time, my whole day seems empty and I don't feel as close to God. It is in those personal times with Him that I feel His love. I know He loves me even when I miss my quiet time, but I don't feel His love." Not everyone would echo this woman's sentiment, but it is certainly true of those individuals whose primary love language is quality time.

Space does not permit a look at scores of others whose primary love language was quality time, but four come to mind: (1) David Brainard, sixteenth-century Yale student and early missionary to Native Americans; (2) E. M. Bounds (1835–1913), a Confederate chaplain, Methodist minister, and author of numerous books, primarily on prayer; (3) Charles Finney (1792–1875), outspoken Presbyterian minister and social activist; and, (4) Praying John Hyde (1865–1912), early missionary to India who well deserved his nickname.[17]

For such people, and others with the love language of quality time, the words of the hymn "In the Garden" by C. Austin Miles are particularly applicable:

I come to the garden alone,
While the dew is still on the roses;
And the voice I hear, falling on my ear,
The Son of God discloses.
He speaks and the sound of His voice
Is so sweet the birds hush their singing,
And the melody that He gave to me
Within my heart is ringing.
And He walks with me, and He talks with me,
And He tells me I am His own;
And the joy we share as we tarry there
None other has ever known.[18]

Those who seek time with God will discover that He is ready and waiting to meet with them. Quality time is a love language that He is always prepared to speak.

QUESTIONS FOR REFLECTION / DISCUSSION

(1) Do you know anyone whom you would guess has the primary love language of quality time? What makes you say so?

(2) One expectation of *every* believer is to spend time with God. What do you think differentiates those with the primary love language of quality time from other believers?

(3) Contrast your spiritual experience with that of someone else you know quite well. Can you see how a difference in primary love languages might cause the experiences to appear quite different, yet equally valid to God?

Chapter Four

GOD SPEAKS LOVE LANGUAGE #3:

GIFTS

Before the days of Interstate 20, it took longer to drive from North Carolina to Texas. Years ago I made that trip to Longview, Texas, after reading the autobiography of R. G. LeTourneau, *Mover of Men and Mountains.* I wanted to meet this engineering genius who had designed his life around a unique partnership with God.

After driving all night, I reached the outskirts of Longview about 9:00 AM. I stopped to refuel and asked the attendant, "Can you tell me how to get to the manufacturing plant owned by R. G. LeTourneau?"

"You mean that rich Christian fool?" the attendant asked.

"Why do you say that?" I responded.

"Because he gives away 90 percent of everything he makes. That doesn't make sense to me."

R. G. LeTourneau didn't make sense to a lot of people. In the 1920s, he had been the laughingstock of highly trained engineers. He went no further in school than eighth grade and never took a course in engineering. Yet by the 1960s he had the distinction of having built the largest earth-moving equipment in the world. His philosophy was, "There are no big jobs; only small machines."[1]

During World War II, his earth-moving machines became the "secret weapons" of the war. After the war, he received the tenth annual award of the National Defense Transportation Association as the person whose "achievement contributed most to the effectiveness of the transportation industry in support of national security."[2] He was a man of dreams with an inventive genius unparalleled by engineers of his day.

LeTourneau attributed all of his success to two factors. First, God had gifted him with the love of machines. He initially feared that his obsession with machines was taking him away from his love of God. But as a young man, he came to understand, "I was just His follower and as long as I . . . didn't get to thinking I was operating under my own head of steam, I was on the right track."[3]

Second, he made a conscious decision to make God his partner in business. Having struggled with the idea of being a missionary, he was challenged by his pastor who said, "God needs businessmen as well as preachers and missionaries." So in the middle of the Great Depression and $100,000 in debt, he pledged $5,000 to his church's missionary efforts.

By the mid-1930s, LeTourneau's small manufacturing operation was beginning to flourish. He erased his debt, and when he realized that profits would be a half million dollars, he told his wife, Evelyn, "I think we've got to do more."

"What's on your mind?" she asked. He explained that in the Old Testament, people were required to tithe their income and added, "Now we aren't compelled to give to God. It's all voluntary. The only thing is, when you consider what God has done for us, we ought to do better for Him out of gratitude than the doubters had to do by law."[4]

Evelyn and he decided to give half of the stock of the company to a foundation. They further agreed to give half of the company's annual earnings to the foundation and to donate half of their own personal income to Christian endeavors around the world. He told his attorney, "I want you to set up a foundation for us. The foundation will sponsor religious, missionary, and educational work for the greater glory of God. I don't know what the laws are, but I want you to fix it so that the funds of the foundation can never be used for company or personal purposes."

His attorney's response? "You're out of your mind, but then you always were."[5]

Eventually LeTourneau would give 90 percent of the common stock of his company to the foundation and 90 percent of his personal income to Christian causes. His many donations funded a Christian camp (in Winona Lake, Indiana), two Christian colleges (in Toccoa, Georgia, and Longview, Texas), and two multimillion-dollar mission projects (one in Liberia and the other in Peru). His life was characterized by giving. His greatest joy came from accomplishing things for God by his giving.

In 1942 the company's net earnings topped the two-million-dollar mark for the first time, and he recalled making his $5,000 pledge to the missions fund while in debt $100,000. When he was asked, "Are you happier now than you were then?" his response was, "More grateful, perhaps, because God has let us help Him do some of the things we wanted to do then. But happier? We had been in the service of the Lord then, and we are in the service of the Lord now, and there is nothing in that kind of happiness that two million net earnings can add to, or buy."[6]

LeTourneau's commitment to giving seemed excessive to many of his peers, but it is not strange to those whose primary love language is gifts. For LeTourneau, it was the most logical thing in the world. He viewed all of life as a gift from God. Time was also viewed as a gift from God to be treated respectfully and gratefully. He once said, "If you waste dollars for me—it is not too serious. I can make that up. But don't waste my time—it can't be recalled."[7]

As a young man, LeTourneau was very reticent to speak publicly, but in his later years he spoke to hundreds of thousands. His speeches always began with the same introduction: "I'm just a mechanic that God has blessed, and He has blessed me—a sinner saved by grace." The word *grace* is a Greek word that literally means "unmerited favor." LeTourneau saw himself "saved" from a life of meaningless activity to one of fruitfulness in cooperating with God as his partner.

The inner peace that came to him at the age of sixteen was the result of God's grace. He explains: "No bolts of lightning hit me. No great flash of awareness. I just prayed to the Lord to save me, and then I was aware of another presence. No words were spoken. I received no messages. It was just that all of my bitterness was drained away, and I was filled with such a vast relief that I could not contain it all. I ran to my mother. 'I'm saved,' I cried."[8]

LeTourneau's missionary efforts were expressions of his love for people that grew out of his personal experience of the love of God. He had a deep concern for the people of the whole world. His questions were always the same: "How much have they got to eat? How comfortably are they housed? What assurance have they got of a life eternal?" He noted in his autobiography, "I know that in the jungles of Africa and South America, the advancements of science make fine reading, but good food, shelter, and the immediate presence of Christ give life its full richness, now and hereafter. I think that is true everywhere."[9]

When one understands that R. G. LeTourneau viewed all of life as an expression of God's love for him, it makes sense why he often said, "The question is not how much of my money I give to God, but rather how much of God's money I keep for myself."[10]

GOD, THE GREAT GIFT-GIVER

LeTourneau's perception of God as the great gift-giver is indeed the God we discover in the Hebrew Old Testament and the Greek New Testament. The opening chapter of the Hebrew Scriptures includes this passage:

> *So God created man in his own image, in the image of God he created him; male and female he created them. . . . Then God said, "I give you every seed-bearing plant on the face of the whole earth and every tree that has fruit with seed in it. They will be yours for food. And to all the beasts of the earth and all the birds of the air and all the creatures that move on the ground—everything that has the breath of life in it—I give every green plant for food." And it was so.*
>
> *God saw all that he had made, and it was very good.[11]*

Compare this picture of God as the "gift-giver" at the dawn of creation with the following words from the last chapter in the Bible, describing the second coming of Jesus Christ and the beginning of a new age:

> *"Behold I am coming soon! My reward is with me. . . . I am the Alpha and the Omega, the First and the Last, the Beginning and the End. Blessed are those who wash their robes, that they may have the right to the tree of life and may go through the gates into the city. . . .*
>
> *"I am the Root and the Offspring of David, and the bright Morning Star."*
>
> *The Spirit and the bride say, "Come!" And let him who hears say,*

"Come!" Whoever is thirsty, let him come; and whoever wishes, let him take the free gift of the water of life.[12]

Throughout the Scriptures—from beginning to end—God reveals Himself as a giver of gifts. Moses said of God: "He will love you and bless you and increase your numbers. He will bless the fruit of your womb, the crops of your land—your grain, new wine and oil—the calves of your herds and the lambs of your flocks in the land that he swore to your forefathers to give you."[13]

Clearly God had established a love relationship with ancient Israel. He provided them with the guidelines to a meaningful and fruitful life. In following those guidelines, they were expressing their trust and love in Jehovah. He, in turn, would shower them with gifts of love.

Israel's reciprocal covenant relationship with God is depicted in the following words of Moses: "So if you faithfully obey the commands I am giving you today—to love the LORD your God and to serve him with all your heart and with all your soul—then I will send rain on your land in its season, both autumn and spring rains, so that you may gather in your grain, new wine and oil. I will provide grass in the fields for your cattle, and you will eat and be satisfied."[14]

This reciprocal love relationship, expressed in giving gifts, is also seen on a personal level. God expressed His love to Solomon, the young king of Israel, by asking, "What shall I give you?"

Solomon requested: "Now, O LORD my God, you have made your servant king in place of my father David. But I am only a little child and do not know how to carry out my duties. . . . So give your servant a discerning heart to govern your people and to distinguish between right and wrong. For who is able to govern this great people of yours?"

God, the great giver of gifts, was pleased with Solomon and responded: "Since you have asked for this and not for long life or wealth for yourself, nor have asked for the death of your enemies but for discernment in administrating justice, I will do what you have asked. I will give you a wise and discerning heart, so that there will never have been anyone like you, nor will there ever be. Moreover, I will give you what you have not asked for—both riches and honor—so that in your lifetime you will have no equal among kings."[15]

Many of the Hebrew songs expressed a similar portrayal of God as the great gift-giver. For example, Psalm 5:12 states: "For surely, O LORD, you bless the righteous; you surround them with your favor as with a shield."

The New Testament continues painting the portrait of the God of love who freely gives gifts to those who love Him. Many agree that the message of the Bible can be summarized in one verse, namely, John 3:16: "For God so loved the world that he gave his one and only Son, that whoever believes in him shall not perish but have eternal life."

It is important to understand that those words were spoken by Jesus as He identified Himself as God's one and only Son and proclaimed His mission on earth. Jesus continued, "For God did not send his Son into the world to condemn the world, but to save the world through him. . . . The Father loves the Son and has placed everything in his hands. Whoever believes in the Son has eternal life, but whoever rejects the Son will not see life, for God's wrath remains on him."[16]

GIFTS PROMISED BY JESUS

The teachings of Jesus were permeated with the concept that God wants to give good gifts to those who love Him. Before Jesus was arrested in Jerusalem, He told His followers, "In a little while you will see me no more, and then after a little while you will see me . . . because I am going to the Father. . . . I tell you the truth, you will weep and mourn while the world rejoices. You will grieve, but your grief will turn to joy."[17]

His message was clear. Jesus was going to die, and after His resurrection He would return to His Father where He had been before His human birth in Bethlehem. But He wanted His followers to know that God would continue to give good gifts to them. He said, "In that day, you will no longer ask me anything. I tell you the truth, my Father will give you whatever you ask in my name. . . . Ask and you will receive, and your joy will be complete."[18]

GIFTS DECLARED BY THE APOSTLES

Much of the New Testament is comprised of letters by the apostle Paul. He began his life as Saul of Tarsus, a well-educated Jewish zealot who wanted to stamp out Christianity in its early stages. He sincerely endeavored to eradicate what he considered to be a violation of the Jewish faith. But after his conversion to Christ, he became an ardent apostle—first to the Jews and then to the Gentiles—proclaiming that Jesus was indeed the Messiah prophesied by Israel's prophets, and that in Him was the gift of eternal life.

Paul's message reflected the covenant love relationship between God and humankind. He wrote, "Be imitators of God, therefore, as dearly loved children and live a life of love, just as Christ loved us and gave himself up for us as a fragrant offering and sacrifice."[19]

Other prominent New Testament figures also described God as the great gift-giver. James wrote: "Every good and perfect gift is from above, coming down from the Father of the heavenly lights, who does not change like shifting shadows." And John noted, "How great is the love the Father has lavished on us, that we should be called the children of God! . . . Dear friends, now we are children of God, and what we will be has not yet been made known. But we know that when he appears, we shall be like him."[20] Perhaps God's greatest gift is the assurance that we will be remade in Christ when He returns.

Throughout human history, God has revealed Himself as one who loves those who will acknowledge Him. He, in turn, expresses His love by giving gifts. Sometimes those gifts are material things that can be touched and tasted, such as food, clothing, and shelter. Other times His gifts are in the realm of the spiritual—eternal life, forgiveness of sins, peace of mind, and purpose of life.

Spiritual gifts were given to the first-century church, especially the early gifts of leadership—"some to be apostles . . . prophets . . . evangelists, and . . . pastors and teachers." Those gifts to the church were to prepare God's people so that the work of Christ on earth could continue.[21]

Since those initial days of the Christian era, every believer in Christ has been given distinct "spiritual gifts," abilities to perform certain tasks in the body of Christ. Such gifts include wisdom, knowledge, faith, gifts of healing, prophecy, distinguishing between spirits, and leadership skills. Spiritual gifts are given by God "for the common good."[22] The various gifts have empowered the followers of Christ to carry on His work for two thousand years.

The theme of God as the giver of gifts runs deeply through the channels of Hebrew and Christian history. To individuals for whom gift-giving is the primary love language, the giving aspect of God's nature is extremely compelling.

"BECAUSE GOD HAS GIVEN SO MUCH TO ME . . ."

Monica was twenty-six when I met her. She attended one of my seminars and responded with a gift: a loaf of freshly baked wheat bread. In the course of our conversation, she said, "Three years ago I was not a Christian. My parents had sent me to church when I was a child, but my father was an alcoholic and my mother was very demanding. Because my parents said they were Christians, I knew that I wanted nothing to do with the church or God. At sixteen I ran away from home and never returned. I lived my life doing what I wanted to do."

For seven years Monica had devoted her life to seeking pleasure, through sex, alcohol, and eventually hard drugs. But she found no happiness and eventually went to a drug treatment center operated by Teen Challenge Ministries.

"It was there where I heard for the first time that God loved me," Monica told me. "I learned that because Jesus had paid the penalty for my sins by dying on the cross, God would forgive me and give me the gift of eternal life. At first I could not believe what I was hearing. I thought of God as the judge who demanded perfection and who cursed those who did not obey His laws. I never pictured Him as a God who loved me and wanted to give me anything. I did not imagine that He could forgive me for all the things I had done, accept me into His family, and let me live forever with Him in heaven. It was too good to be true. I resisted the idea for several weeks.

"As I read the Scriptures for myself, one night I cried out to God and said, 'If it is true, if You really love me, then I'm asking You to forgive me and I'm inviting You into my life. If You can clean up my life and deliver me from drug addiction and give me the gift of eternal life, I am willing to accept Your love.' My life changed that night, and I know I will never be the same again."

Monica completed the program, and Teen Challenge referred her to a group of Christians who invited her to live with them. She found they genuinely cared for each other. She described how two weeks later, "they gave me the first birthday cake I had had since I was twelve. Here were people, themselves former addicts, who had accepted God's love and were now giving His love to others."

Monica met Jim there; they fell in love and were married a year before she attended my seminar. With her gift came an explanation: "Because God has given so much to me, my ministry is baking bread and giving it to others. Every week I bake twenty loaves of bread and distribute them to people God brings into my life."

I embraced Monica and Jim, thanked God for His gifts to them, and then prayed His blessing upon their marriage. Monica is a living example that God speaks the love language of gifts.

Throughout history, thousands of individuals whose primary love language is gifts have been drawn to God because He stands not as a judge to condemn but as a Father who bestows forgiveness and eternal life to those who will receive His love.

I think of Maria, a young wife in California, who said to me, "When I read your book, *The Five Love Languages,* I was especially attracted to the chapter on gifts because that is my primary love language. I started thinking about other people whose love language might be gifts.

"I remembered the pastor of our first church when we moved to California. He gave us a piano the first month we arrived at the church. He regularly brought vegetables to our house. He was always asking, 'What do you need?' It seemed he couldn't give us enough.

"I knew his love language was gifts, and we were the recipients of his love. When we would say 'Thank you,' he would say, 'Don't thank me; thank God. All good gifts come from Him.'"

It was clear to me that Maria's pastor was expressing his love to God when he gave gifts to people in his congregation. I suspect that if I could have talked with him, he would probably have quoted the words of Jesus:

"Then the King will say to those on his right, 'Come, you who are blessed by my Father; take your inheritance, the kingdom prepared for you since the creation of the world. For I was hungry and you gave me something to

eat, I was thirsty and you gave me something to drink, I was a stranger and you invited me in, I needed clothes and you clothed me, I was sick and you looked after me, I was in prison and you came to visit me.'

"Then the righteous will answer him, 'Lord, when did we see you hungry and feed you, or thirsty and give you something to drink? When did we see you a stranger and invite you in, or needing clothes and clothe you? When did we see you sick or in prison and go to visit you?'

"The King will reply, 'I tell you the truth, whatever you did for one of the least of these brothers of mine, you did for me.'" [23]

The message of Jesus was clear. One of the ways of expressing love to God is by giving gifts to those who need them. It is this truth that deeply motivates followers of Jesus. As one man said to me, "I never feel more joy than when I am giving to others. I feel like this is why God has given to me, and it is the way I can express my love to Him." Another man said, "I feel closest to God when I am taking care of His people by giving them what they cannot provide for themselves."

When I think of giving gifts as an expression of one's love for God, the first person who comes to my mind is Anne Wenger. I knew her for over twenty-five years. She was a speech pathologist who had suffered from polio and walked haltingly. When she retired from public work, people would take their children to her house for speech therapy. She gave freely of her time and expertise, and no child ever left her house without a gift—perhaps a piece of literature she thought would be helpful or an apple from the fruit basket in the kitchen near her chair.

A young college student who lived in the basement apartment mowed Anne's grass. Others from the church volunteered to vacuum her floors and mop the kitchen. The youth group raked her leaves each fall. Everyone was happy to do something for Anne, perhaps to reciprocate for her gifts.

I can attest that I never left Anne's presence without something in my hand, usually a book or booklet that she thought would help in my ministry to others. I remember one of the last times I visited in her home, a few weeks before she went to live in a nursing facility. She said, "I'm giving away my possessions while I'm still alive because I want them to go to people whom I think will use them. I want your son Derek to have this set of books." She pointed to a thirty-five-volume set, the Library of the World's Best Literature.

I said to her, "Anne, I know he would be happy to receive the books, but I want you to check with your daughter first and make sure that she doesn't want them."

Anne nodded and said, "You're right. That's a good idea. Let me ask Elizabeth." Two weeks later I got a call from Anne to come and pick up the books.

Even in the nursing home, Anne's pattern of giving did not waver. She had almost no material possessions at that point, yet as I got ready to leave her room, she would say, "Here, take this lotion home to Karolyn. I know she can use it." And she would give me a small container of lotion, probably one that had been given to her by someone else.

Anne Wenger was a giver who is remembered by hundreds of individuals who received tokens of her love through the years. In my conversations with Anne over twenty-five years, she spoke deeply of the love of God that she had experienced. She saw God as the great gift-giver, and her gifts to others were a reflection of His love through her.

HOW WE RECEIVE GIFTS FROM GOD

How does someone receive God's gift of love? Some gifts are given indiscriminately by God to everyone, such as the rising and setting of the sun, the gentle rain, spring flowers, the songs of birds, and the seasons. The psalmist wrote, "The heavens declare the glory of God;

the skies proclaim the work of his hands. Day after day they pour forth speech; night after night they display knowledge. There is no speech or language where their voice is not heard."[24]

As parents provide for the basic needs of their children—food, clothing, and shelter—so God provides for His children day after day. However, other gifts of God are reserved for those who ask.

Jesus once said, "Ask and it will be given to you; seek and you will find; knock and the door will be opened to you. For everyone who asks receives; he who seeks finds; and to him who knocks, the door will be opened." Then Jesus explained *why* we could count on God to give us good gifts. "Which of you, if his son asks for bread, will give him a stone? Or if he asks for a fish, will give him a snake? If you, then, though you are evil, know how to give good gifts to your children, how much more will your Father in heaven give good gifts to those who ask him!"[25]

I have always found it astounding that the eternal God would invite people to ask Him for gifts, but that is precisely what Jesus taught. That does not mean that God will give us exactly what we ask for, every time we ask. A wise parent will not give a child three candy bars even though the child may ask. The promise is that God will give "good gifts" when asked. Parents would not give a child something they knew to be destructive even though the child asked intently, nor would God. He loves us too much for that.

The epistle of James also indicates another reason God does not always give us exactly what we ask. "When you ask, you do not receive, because you ask with wrong motives, that you may spend what you get on your pleasures."[26] Hedonistic requests that focus on selfish pleasure will not be answered by God. He loves us too much to allow us to build our lives on a faulty premise.

In a proper relationship with God, our desire is to receive gifts from Him that will enable us to give to others. Thus, a pastor asks for wisdom in shepherding his flock; a parent asks for emotional and physical strength to support his or her children. If we ask for material possessions (which is not discouraged in the Scriptures), it is for the purpose of using them to enhance our ministry to others. Requesting material things simply for the sake of possessing them is foreign to the biblical concept of love. Sincere followers of Jesus always ask: "How may I use what God gives me to minister to others?"

A parent may pray for tuition money to send a child to college. When it comes, the money is invested in enriching the child's life. If God provides more than is needed, it can be used to enrich the life of someone else's child. After the needs of the family are met, any other available funds can be given to support the work of missionaries and pastors around the world.

God's abundant gifts to us are yet another expression of His love, and we reflect that love by loving others. We receive the gifts of wisdom, insight, experience, expertise, and material possessions to enrich the lives of other people. God's gifts are never given because we deserve them; they are given as expressions of His love for us. Thus, our gifts to others are not based upon the person's performance or what the individual has done for us, but rather flow from our love for the person.

QUESTIONS FOR REFLECTION / DISCUSSION

(1) Who are some people you know who appear to have gift giving as a primary love language? In what ways do they show the love of God through giving? Do you aspire to be like such people, or do you think they have a special ability to give that isn't available to everyone?

(2) What are some of the gifts of God you have received lately without even asking? What gifts would you like to ask for specifically? How would those things be used for the benefit of others as well as yourself?

(3) When you consider that giving can include much more than money and other tangible things, do you see any new opportunities to speak this love language?

(4) What are some ways you can use the gifts God has given you to give back to God (either tangibly or spiritually)?

Chapter Five

GOD SPEAKS LOVE LANGUAGE #4:

ACTS *of* SERVICE

It was the week between Christmas and New Year's Day, and Paul Brown (not his real name) was in my office for his annual "checkup." For over fifteen years, Paul had called my secretary and asked for an appointment the week after Christmas. He was a high school math teacher in another city who spent part of his week of freedom with me.

He looked the same as last year and began as he always begins: "How's your son? . . . How's your daughter? . . . How's your wife?" His interest was sincere and he listened as I gave my report.

Then he said what he always says: "Well, let's cut to the chase." He pulled a piece of crumpled paper from one pocket and a pen from the other, and he asked me the same question he always asks: "How do you know when it's God's will for you to get married?"

Paul is forty-two and has never been married, though he had been dating Becky for twelve years, and they were friends seven years before they started dating. "Why do you ask that question?" I inquired, with a clinical look on my face.

"Well, Becky has told me not to bother coming around anymore if I'm not willing to talk marriage. I don't know if I'm ready for that. My lifestyle doesn't lend itself to marriage. I work seventy-five hours a week, and I don't think most wives would put up with that."

I nodded and asked, "Tell me your daily schedule."

"Well, officially my day starts at 8:30 AM, but I usually get there an hour earlier. I teach from 8:30 till 3:30, and then I tutor individual students from 3:30 till 10:30 at night and sometimes later. Some of the kids I'm assigned can't do basic math. It's not cool to ask questions in class so they act like they understand when they don't. They can't graduate from high school without passing the algebra exam, and they will never do that without individual help. They are the kind of kids that aren't going to understand in the classroom; but when I get them one-on-one, there's no faking it, and they learn.

"I don't mind putting in the time. Of course, I don't get paid for it, and I don't think a wife would understand."

Paul had been keeping this schedule for seven years. None of the other math teachers did, of course. But as he explained, "They have the cream of the crop. They explain a concept in class, and their students get it, but my students don't. I'm dealing with kids who don't understand the basics. They're still trying to figure out which way to move the decimal if you want to go to a percentage. Is it left or right?

"Let me tell you something God gave me," Paul continued. "It just came to me one day. I prayed, 'Lord, how can I help these students understand and remember which way to move the decimal?' So I wrote the alphabet on the board—A, B, C, D . . . right on down through P. I underlined D and P. I pointed to the D and said, 'Now, if you've got a decimal and you want to make it a percentage (I pointed to the P), which way do you move the decimal?'

"They said, 'To the right.' Then I went to the P and said, 'If you've got a percentage and you want to translate it to a decimal, which way do you move the decimal?' I pointed to the D.

"'To the left,' they shouted. I knew they had it. And when I got their exams three weeks later, they actually had the alphabet written across the top of the exam paper with the D and the P underlined."

We both laughed. Paul continued, "It's a challenge, but I know I'm making a difference in their lives. They will graduate from high school because I took the time to help them. I don't have any discipline problems in my classroom. The students know I am on their side. They tell each other, 'Don't bother Mr. B; he's one of us.'"

I said, "Paul, I think you're right. I don't think any wife would be happy with her husband working seventy-five hours a week. So let's imagine that you are married and had to cut back the hours. What would be the possibilities?"

"Well, I'd need a full-time assistant who could tutor the students after class. In fact, I told the principal one time that he needed to hire me as a full-time tutor. Somebody else could teach the classes, and I would work from 3:30 until 11:30 PM every day, tutoring the students who can't get it in class. I know that's not going to happen, but it would be ideal.

"The other thing I've thought about is teaching math in a college prep school or on the college level. I know my school will never move me because the principal is happy with the test scores, and so are the parents. They know that no one else will invest the time I spend with the students. But I'm not sure I want to be transferred. After all, this is what motivated me to go back to the university and get my master's degree. You remember?" He looked at me and I nodded.

I remembered. In fact, I remembered a lot about Paul. I remembered when he was in high school and his mother had died with cancer after praying that God would take care of her seven children. I remembered when he went off to college to pursue his vision of becoming a math teacher; it was there where he became a devoted follower of Jesus Christ. I remembered when Paul changed his major from math to communications, a decision made out of a sincere desire to learn how to communicate the teachings of Christ to others. I remembered the struggles he went through for several years after college, working for a communications company but always wondering if this was really what he should be doing with his life. And I remembered distinctly his choice to return to the university to finish his major in math and pursue a master's degree so he could teach—his original vision and passion.

I explained that Paul's dilemma was similar to that of thousands of priests and nuns through the years. In his case, he had devoted his life to teaching math and helping students graduate from high school who otherwise would not make it. He was making a difference in their lives forever. On the other hand, he had a desire for marriage, but didn't see the two as compatible.

I paused and continued, "Maybe it's time for you to realistically explore the possibility of marriage. You could suggest to Becky, 'I'm willing to discuss marriage if both of us realize that the process may not lead to a wedding.' You might attend some marriage preparation classes. You could take a psychological test to indicate the level of compatibility between the two of you. You should look at your lifestyles and consider what things would be like if you were married. And you can discuss the possibility of exploring change in vocational settings. But at the end of the process, you could make an intelligent decision about marriage."

The room fell silent. I could tell that Paul was contemplating what I had just said. "I'm not sure I'm willing to take those steps," he finally replied. "At least, not at this time." We talked about several other matters of lesser importance. As usual, Paul thanked me for my time and told me how much he appreciated my being a sounding board. As he walked out, I knew I would see him again next Christmas. Once more we would talk about "how to know the will of God about marriage."

Paul's primary love language is acts of service. Tutoring those underachieving math students was his way of expressing his love to God. The thought of walking away from those students, even for the prospect of a marriage relationship, was difficult for Paul to imagine.

This had not been the first time I had observed Paul's love language. While he was working for the communications company, he volunteered to run the sound system for his church and to edit the pastor's sermons for local radio—consistently spending twenty hours a week in this volunteer service. It was another way of expressing his love to God.

I cannot predict whether Paul will ever get married, but I *can* predict that if he does he will find a way to serve others, because acts of service is his primary love language.

"THE WORK IS A MEANS TO EXPRESS OUR LOVE FOR HIM": MOTHER TERESA

A much better known example of someone with the primary love language of acts of service is Mother Teresa. As a teenager, Agnes Bojaxhiu (Mother Teresa's birth name) joined a Catholic youth group in the Jesuit parish of the Sacred Heart in her hometown of Skopje, Albania. At the age of eighteen, she moved to Ireland to join the Sisters of Our Lady of Loreto. Three months later she was sent to Calcutta, India, and later to Darjeeling, near the Himalayas, where in 1937 she made permanent vows and took the name "Teresa."

After nine years of teaching at the only Catholic school for girls in Calcutta, most of whom were from well-to-do families, Sister Teresa became aware of a different calling. She said, "I had to leave the convent

(Loreto) and consecrate myself to help the poor, living among them. Abandoning Loreto was an even harder sacrifice than leaving my family that first time in order to follow my vocation. But I had to do it. It was a calling. I knew I had to go; I did not know how to get there."[1]

Some of Mother Teresa's former students followed her, and they formed the nucleus of what became "Missionaries of Charity." Mother Teresa started working with those she found first: abandoned children living in the city parks. She began by teaching them basic habits of good hygiene. She helped them learn the alphabet. She had no master blueprint for her work, but her goal was clear: to love and serve the poor, seeing Jesus in them. She said, "In determining which work would be done, there was no planning at all. I headed the work in accordance with how I felt called by the people's sufferings. God made me see what He wanted me to do."[2]

When she found a woman dying on a sidewalk, she took the woman home with her and shortly thereafter opened the Home for the Dying in order to provide a peaceful and dignified place for people to die. Later, when she found abandoned children, sometimes the sons and daughters of those staying at the Home for the Dying, she opened Shishu Bhavan, the first of a series of children's homes. In similar manner, she started homes for lepers, people with AIDS, and unwed mothers. Awarded the Nobel Peace Prize in 1979, she did not consider the cash award as personal property but accepted it in the name of the poor and spent it all on them.

To view Mother Teresa as simply an unusually altruistic person is to miss the central message of her life. As she explained: "Whoever the poorest of the poor are, they are Christ for us—Christ under the guise of human suffering. The Missionaries of Charity are firmly convinced that each time we offer help to the poor, we really offer help to Christ." On another occasion she said, "When we touch the sick and needy, we touch the suffering body of Christ." And again, "Jesus is the one we take care of, visit, clothe, feed, and comfort. Every time we do this for the poorest of the poor, to the sick, to the dying, to the lepers, and to the ones who suffer from AIDS, we should not serve the poor like they *were* Jesus; we should serve the poor because they are Jesus."[3]

The central dimension of Mother Teresa's acts of service was spiritual in nature. "To me, Jesus is the Life I want to live, the Light I want to reflect, the Way to the Father, the Love I want to express, the Joy I want to share, the Peace I want to sow around me."[4] For her, loving God meant serving people.

In addition to service, love meant sacrifice for Mother Teresa. After all, she reasoned, that was how God expressed His love to us: "True love causes pain. Jesus, in order to give us the proof of His love, died on the cross. A mother, in order to give birth to her baby, has to suffer. If you really love one another, you will not be able to avoid making sacrifices."[5]

When Mother Teresa challenged others to join her in loving God, her invitation was most often expressed in terms of acts of service. "I invite all those who appreciate our work to look around them and be willing to love those who have no love and to offer them their services. Are we not, by definition, messengers of love?" Later she said, "Let us not be satisfied just by giving money. Money is not everything. The poor need the work of our hands, the love of our hearts. Love, an abundant love, is the expression of our Christian religion."[6]

To those who sought to follow her example, Mother Teresa emphasized the connection between loving people and loving God.

It happened once, when the Congregation of the Missionary Brothers of Charity was first established, that a young Brother came to me and said, "Mother, I have a special call to work with the lepers. I want to give my life to them, my whole being. Nothing attracts me more than that." I know for a fact that he truly loved those afflicted with leprosy. I, in turn, answered him, "I think that you are somewhat wrong, Brother. Our vocation consists in belonging to Jesus. The work is nothing but a means to express our love for him. The work in itself is not important. What is important is for you to belong to Jesus and he is the one who offers you the means to express that belonging."[7]

Mother Teresa realized that caring for spiritual needs was even more important than caring for material needs: "We have the specific task of giving material and spiritual help to the poorest of the poor, not only the ones in the slums but those who live in any corner of the world as well. . . . If our work were just to wash and feed and give medicines to the sick, the center would have closed a long time ago. The most important thing in our centers is the opportunity we are offered to reach the souls."[8]

THE SUPREME ACT OF SERVICE: A LIFE SACRIFICED

God expressed His love for humankind by sending His uniquely begotten Son, Jesus, who in turn expressed His love by the supreme act of service: giving His life for people's sins. When Agnes Bojaxhiu responded to that love as a young teenage girl, she began a life course of faithfulness and distinction. Her transformation into Mother Teresa seems incredible to many people, yet the God she worshiped is more than capable of such a change. He is the God of Abraham, Isaac, Jacob, and Joseph. The Bible declares Him to be "the God and Father of our Lord Jesus Christ."[9] And He speaks fluently the love language acts of service.

What Jewish child does not know the story of God's deliverance of Israel from Egyptian bondage? So important is that act of love that the

Jewish community has celebrated it at Passover for over 3,500 years. During their forty-year journey from Egypt to Canaan, the people of Israel watched God express His love by acts of service on numerous occasions, including parting the Red Sea and providing food and water in the wilderness.

Unlike Baal and the pagan gods of their neighbors, who never responded to the prayers and sacrifices of those who called on them, Israel's God revealed His love by acts of service in response to the prayers of His people. Enemies were routed, plagues were averted, droughts were ended, and diseases healed when Israel called on God. The perception of God as One who acts was so central to Jewish thought that one of the names they attributed to Him was *Elohim,* the all-powerful One. The Jewish nation was so profoundly affected by God's love through acts of service that they often depicted their history by reciting the mighty acts of God on behalf of Israel.

For example, the psalmist wrote of pagan gods, "Their idols are silver and gold, made by the hands of men. They have mouths, but cannot speak, eyes, but they cannot see; they have ears, but cannot hear, noses, but they cannot smell; they have hands, but cannot feel, feet, but they cannot walk; nor can they utter a sound with their throats." In contrast, speaking of the God of Israel, he wrote, "O house of Israel, trust in the LORD—he is [our] help and shield. . . . The LORD remembers us and will bless us: he will bless the house of Israel, he will bless the house of Aaron, he will bless those who fear the LORD—small and great alike."[10]

Clearly, the God of Israel expressed His love by acts of service to those who called upon Him. And while many people accept this fact about God, a significant number are reluctant to believe the same about Jesus. Yet when we examine the life of Jesus of Nazareth, we find Him identifying with the God of Israel. The claims are so clear and so woven into Jesus' concept of Himself that many have found them incredible and have concluded that Jesus was a man with delusions of grandeur, one not to be seriously considered as a creditable religious leader.

Early in His adult life, Jesus returned to the village of Nazareth where He had grown up, and went to the synagogue on the Sabbath. When asked to read the Scriptures, He opened the scroll to Isaiah 61 and read: "The Spirit of the Lord is on me, because he has anointed me to preach good news to the poor. He has sent me to proclaim freedom for the prisoners and recovery of sight for the blind, to release the oppressed, to proclaim the year of the Lord's favor."[11]

This passage was commonly understood to be a prophecy of the Messiah who would someday come to Israel. When Jesus completed the reading He said: "Today this scripture is fulfilled in your hearing." Thus, He claimed to be the long-awaited Messiah. So furious were the leaders of the synagogue that they literally forced Jesus out of town, which led Him to say, "No prophet is accepted in his hometown."[12]

On another occasion, Jesus looked toward heaven and prayed: "Father, the time has come. Glorify your Son, that your Son may glorify you. For you granted him authority over all people that he might give eternal life to all those you have given him." Then He added these words to His sincere prayer: "Now this is eternal life: that they may know you, the only true God, and Jesus Christ, whom you have sent. I have brought you glory on earth by completing the work you gave me to do. And now, Father, glorify me in your presence with the glory I had with you before the world began."[13]

Jesus had declared Himself God's unique Son who had been given great glory in heaven. Later, seeking to prepare His followers for His God-ordained death, Jesus said:

"Do not let your hearts be troubled. Trust in God; trust also in me. In my Father's house are many rooms; if it were not so, I would have told you. I am going there to prepare a place for you. And if I go and prepare a place for you, I will come back and take you to be with me that you also may be where I am. You know the way to the place where I am going."

Thomas said to him, "Lord, we don't know where you are going, so how can we know the way?"

Jesus answered, "I am the way and the truth and the life. No one comes to the Father except through me. If you really knew me, you would know my Father as well." [14]

Jesus claimed His "acts of service," which included preparing "a place" for His followers, were like the loving acts of service by His Father. But even His disciples had trouble understanding the connection between Jesus and God the Father:

Philip said, "Lord, show us the Father and that will be enough for us."

Jesus answered: "Don't you know me, Philip, even after I have been among you such a long time? Anyone who has seen me has seen the Father. How can you say, 'Show us the Father'? Don't you believe that I am in the Father, and that the Father is in me? The words I say to you are not just my own. Rather, it is the Father living in me who is doing his work. Believe me when I say that I am in the Father and the Father is in me; or at least believe on the evidence of the miracles themselves." [15]

If someone begins with the assumption that the incarnation—God becoming man—is impossible, then it is easy to see why he or she would find Jesus' teachings to be incredible. Yet it is interesting that Jesus used His acts of service as evidence of the truthfulness of His claims. He told His disciples, "If I had not done among them what no one else did, they would not be guilty of sin. But now they have seen these miracles, and yet they have hated both me and my Father. But this is to fulfill what is written in their Law: 'They hated me without reason.'" [16]

RESPONDING TO JESUS' ACTS OF SERVICE

The miracles that Jesus performed were never capricious. They were always expressions of His love for people. Healing the sick, giving sight to the blind, calming the storm, casting out demons—those were not only supernatural feats that identified Him with God, but also expressions of His love. On three occasions He even brought a dead person back to life.[17] Such acts of service were reflected in His statement, "As the Father has loved me, so have I loved you."[18]

Jesus framed His own death as an act of service when He said, "My command is this: Love each other as I have loved you. Greater love has no one than this, that he lay down his life for his friends." His love was further evidenced when He said from the cross as He was dying, "Father, forgive them, for they do not know what they are doing."[19]

Paul the apostle clearly understood the death of Christ as an expression of God's love. Here are his words written to the church in Rome: "You see, at just the right time, when we were still powerless, Christ died for the ungodly. Very rarely will anyone die for a righteous man, though for a good man someone might possibly dare to die. But God demonstrates his own love for us in this: While we were still sinners, Christ died for us."[20] Paul was overwhelmed by the thought that Christ would die not for good people, but for sinners.

Another clear connection between Jesus and God the Father was indicated by an earlier prayer of Jesus: "Father, I want those you have given me to be with me where I am, and to see my glory, the glory you have given me because you loved me before the creation of the world. I have made you known to them, and will continue to make you known in order that the love you have for me may be in them and that I myself may be in them."[21]

Jesus regularly identified with God the Father. He referred to being with God before the world was created. He taught that He came into the world from the Father. His message was clear that He was returning to the Father after His death and resurrection. His regular acts of service for other people reflected those of God as recorded in Old Testament Scripture.

Such facts have forced people who wish to be intellectually honest to conclude that there are only three possibilities. Jesus must be: (1) a deliberate deceiver to be ignored; (2) a deluded peasant to be pitied; or (3) the divine Lord to be worshiped. There are no intellectual grounds for considering Him a great religious teacher. His claims of deity do not give us that alternative.

C. S. Lewis spelled out these options in his classic book, *Mere Christianity*:

> I am trying here to prevent anyone saying the really foolish thing that people often say about Him: "I'm ready to accept Jesus as a great moral teacher, but I don't accept his claim to be God." That is the one thing we must not say. A man who was merely a man and said the sort of things Jesus said would not be a great moral teacher. He would either be a lunatic—on a level with the man who says he is a poached egg—or else he would be the Devil of Hell. You must make your choice. Either this man was, and is, the Son of God: or else a madman or something worse. You can shut Him up for a fool, you can spit at Him and kill Him as a demon; or you can fall at His feet and call Him Lord and God. But let us not come with any patronising nonsense about

His being a great human teacher. He has not left that open to us. He did not intend to.[22]

For all who examine the life of Jesus, He becomes a fork in the road of life. Many choose the path of submission—they bow the knee, submit the heart, and arise to walk humbly as His servants. Of that group, many testify that what ultimately won their hearts was His love expressed by miraculous acts of service, from the humility of His human birth to His sacrificial, voluntary death that paid the penalty for their sins. And serving a God who speaks through acts of service is ample motivation for them to serve one another as well.

QUESTIONS FOR REFLECTION/DISCUSSION

(1) Do you know anyone like "Paul Brown," who places acts of service above everything else—even his or her own personal benefit? To what extent does the person's Christian commitment motivate him or her?

(2) If someone like Mother Teresa spent time in your neighborhood, what needs do you think he or she would see that most others regularly overlook?

(3) How many volunteer organizations can you name in your area that exist primarily to offer acts of service to others? (Meals on Wheels? Goodwill? Programs of local churches?) Are there things you can do to get involved with one or more such services?

(4) On a personal level, what acts of service have you done for others lately? Can you think of any opportunities you missed?

Chapter Six

GOD SPEAKS LOVE LANGUAGE #5:

PHYSICAL TOUCH

A few years ago I was in southern Germany to lead a marriage seminar one weekend and a parenting seminar the next. Karl was my interpreter for both events, and in all my travels I have never had a more enthusiastic interpreter.

From my first lecture, I could tell it was going to be fun. As I entered into the personalities of the characters in my stories, Karl joined me. When I crescendoed, he crescendoed. When I went into falsetto, Karl went into falsetto. When I moved my hands, he moved his hands. When I got intense, his eyes tightened as he followed me. When I broke into laughter, he laughed. At times I found myself laughing as he mimicked me.

About half of the audience understood English, so they laughed when I finished the story. The other half laughed when Karl finished the story. It was exciting!

During the breaks in the seminars, Karl served as my interpreter in personal conversations with those who were attending. He and I also had considerable time to talk with each other. Seven of my books had been translated into German. Karl was familiar with *The Five Love Languages* and was especially interested in that particular lecture. He told me that his love language was definitely physical touch. Affectionate touches by his wife spoke deeply to him.

By the middle of the second seminar I was getting to know Karl pretty well. At that point he asked me, "What book are you writing now?" I told him, "I'm writing a book on the love languages of God. It is my hypothesis that people experience God's love more deeply when God speaks in their primary love language. For example, if a person's primary love language is words of affirmation, he or she will experience God's love more deeply when it comes through words."

I gave Karl the illustration of a young man who weeks earlier told me he came to God after stopping at a small hotel. He had become alienated from both parents and had little money.

"In desperation I picked up the Gideon Bible in my room," the traveler had told me. "It opened to Jeremiah chapter 31 and I read, 'I have loved you with an everlasting love; I have drawn you with loving-kindness.' And a few verses later, 'He who scattered Israel will gather them and will watch over his flock like a shepherd.'

"I know the prophet was writing those words to Israel," the man had told me, "but that night they were God's words to me. I came back to God, and the next day returned home to my parents."

I explained to Karl that the power of God's words had spoken deeply to the traveler's spirit; God had spoken his primary love language.

I noticed that Karl could hardly wait for me to finish my illustration. With great emotion he said, "That is certainly true of me. I told you last weekend that my primary love language is physical touch. Let me tell you how I came to be a Christian. I was seventeen years old. I wasn't sure there was a God, but if there was, I knew I wanted to know Him. I was riding my bicycle one night right after dark. I had a cigarette in my hand. I had been smoking since I was thirteen. I knew it wasn't good for me and I really wanted to quit. I had tried several times unsuccessfully. I looked down at my cigarette and said aloud, 'God, if You really exist, then take these cigarettes away from me.' Immediately, it was like a huge hand came out of nowhere, slapped my hand, and my cigarette was gone.

"I stopped my bicycle, and it was like the arms of God wrapped around me. I felt His presence and wept. I knew that not only did God exist but also that God loved me. From that day I have been a follower of Jesus. He spoke my love language.

"He touched me then," Karl said, "and He still touches me. Not always, but often when I'm praying and singing, I can feel His presence. I know that God is a spirit, but when His Spirit touches my spirit, I feel it in my body. That is when I feel closest to God."

FEELING THE PRESENCE OF GOD

Karl's experience is not unusual. People whose primary love language is physical touch often speak of "feeling the presence of God." I wrote of Greta's story in chapter 3 and briefly mentioned her husband, Rod. He was the one who made the God connection the second Sunday he attended a charismatic church. A friend had asked if he would like to go to the front of the church after the service and have people pray for him. Not wanting to offend his friend, he agreed.

Several men gathered around him and began to pray aloud. Rod said to me, "I had never experienced anything like it. Within a few minutes I was weeping uncontrollably and praying aloud myself, asking God to forgive me. God touched me that day. It was like electricity running through my body, and I felt totally clean."

Later in my conversation with Rod he had told me, "That was the beginning, but God has touched me many times since. Just recently I was having a difficult time at work. Emotionally I was low. I was feeling disconnected from Greta. As I was driving down the road I said to God, 'I need You; I really need You.' Immediately I was overcome by the presence of God. It was like He was there with me in the car. I started weeping and had to pull off the road. I must have sat there fifteen minutes, weeping and praising God. I was overcome with joy and peace, and I knew that God was going to help me.

"I don't have those experiences with God very often," Rod continued. "I guess that's good. I'm not sure my body could handle it. But when they happen, it is sheer joy. Those are the highest moments in my life, when I know that I'm in the presence of God."

I replied, "What I hear you saying is that these deep physical, emotional experiences with God come only periodically. So in the normal flow of your life, when do you feel closest to God?"

"When I'm singing praise songs I often feel God's presence," Rod said. "I can be at church or alone. It's like His presence passes by and I feel it like the wind. Sometimes I weep while I sing, but they are tears of joy. I know that God is there and I'm singing praise to Him."

As Rod told me about his experiences with God, my mind flashed to the island nation of Singapore, where I had visited some months earlier. One night I sat in a worship service at which I had been invited to speak. The congregational singing was being led by a small group of "praise singers," young people who appeared to be teenagers. As they sang, several began to raise their hands and eyes toward heaven. Tears began to flow down their faces as they sang praises to God.

After the service, I asked one of the ministers who the young people were. He said, "Those are young people who have been saved off the streets. They love God intently and they love to sing His praises."

As he told me that, my clinical mind began to paint a picture. Here were young people who had never known the warm embrace of a father's arms and who had been abandoned by their mothers. Yet they were experiencing the touch of a heavenly Father who has revealed Himself as "a father to the fatherless." They identified with the Hebrew songwriter who wrote, "Though my father and mother forsake me, the LORD will receive me."[1]

Later, I recalled that not all of the young "praise singers" were weeping or raising their hands heavenward. Some gave no evidence of being physically moved, but I had no reason to doubt that their praise was sincere. I was relatively sure that those who wept had experienced the love of God most deeply through a conscious awareness of His presence. He touched them, and they felt His warm embrace. Feeling deeply loved by God, they reciprocated with raised hands and flowing tears.

TOUCH, COMPASSION, AND FERVENT PRAYER

Some months later, I was back in America visiting an inner-city "house church" comprised of young followers of Jesus who had never been inside a traditional Christian church. They were in their late teens and early twenties, and had grown up with a totally secular worldview. Most of them had been involved with sex, alcohol, and drugs from their early teenage years. Many had grown up in foster homes. More than half of them had never known their fathers. Before coming to the house church, they had slept in the city park or under bridges if the weather was inclement.

Yet, through the ministry of this house church they had become followers of Jesus. They had found not only deliverance from their addictions, but "family" as well. They had discovered the truth expressed in Psalm 68:6: "God sets the lonely in families, he leads forth the prisoners with singing."

It was in this setting where I met Nicholas, a young man whose height, facial features, and hair reminded me of my own son. He appeared somewhat older than the rest of the group. I started a conversation and he soon began to open up.

"I spent the first eighteen years of my life living on the streets of Chicago," he said. "Then I moved west. I ended up here, where I have been for the last ten years. I was sleeping in the park and washing dishes at a restaurant when a friend invited me to a rave. What I didn't know at the time was that it was a Christian rave. All night long we danced to the music, but periodically members of the band would talk about their own spiritual journeys.

"It took awhile, but I began to realize that they were all talking about God. It was strange to me. I had never heard anyone talk about God unless they were cursing, but God seemed to have made a difference in these people's lives. About four o'clock in the morning one of them said, 'If you would like someone to pray with you, come over to this end of the building.' I had never had anyone pray for me, so I thought it might be a good experience. I worked my way to that side of the building. I was met by this guy and gal who put their hands on my shoulder and said, 'Would you like to pray?'

"'I don't know how to pray,' I said.

"'We'll pray for you,' they replied. So I sat down in a chair. They got on their knees, placed their hands on my shoulders, and both of them prayed for me. At the time I didn't know what was happening to me. I thought I was going crazy. Now I know God was touching my life and changing me. I felt a presence that I've never felt before, and I saw Jesus standing in front of me saying, 'I love you. I've always loved you. I want you to be My child. I want you to be My son. I want you to follow Me.' I didn't know who He was, so I asked, 'Who are You?' And He said, 'I'm Jesus. I'm God's Son. I know you don't have a family. I want to be your

Brother, and God wants to be your Father. These people who are praying for you are working for Me. They love you too, and they'll help you. Listen to them.'"

Nicholas had answered, "OK. I will." When he did, he felt a heavy load lifted off his shoulders. He began to cry and to say, "Thank You, Jesus; thank You, Jesus; thank You, Jesus." The next morning Nicholas accepted an offer to live with the couple who had prayed with him and some other people in the house church.

He said, "At the time I just thought it was a religious group of some kind. But I've been here three years now, and they have been the best years of my life. God has delivered me from drugs, and for the first time in my life I have a family. Jesus has changed my life, and if He can change my life, He can change anybody's life."

I spent three days with this house church and discovered that prayer was more than a ritual for them. My first night there a young girl came in who was obviously pregnant and appeared to be delusional. The first response of the leaders of the group was, "Let's pray for her." Six or eight of the people who were in the house at the time gathered around her, each of them placing one hand upon her with the other hand clasping a fellow pray-er. My hand was joined with Nicholas's. One by one they began to pray for her.

They prayed with a love and intensity that I've seldom seen in a traditional church. When one was praying aloud, the others were supportive, saying, "Yes, Lord," "Amen," "Thank You, Jesus," and "Lord, have mercy."

When Nicholas began to pray, his hand, which I was holding, began to tremble. As he continued to pray, the shake became more pronounced. When the prayer was over, the group stood, hugged each other, hugged the young lady, and expressed praise to God for answering their prayers. Then they took the young lady to the kitchen and fed her.

Later that evening, when they discovered she had no place to go, they invited her to spend the night.

The next day Nicholas and I were on the street doing what they called a "prayer walk." The group members would walk down the street praying (sometimes aloud, sometimes silently) for the people they passed and for those who lived and worked in the surrounding buildings. I took the opportunity to tell Nicholas that I had never prayed with anyone whose hands shook as they prayed. "Oh, really?" he said. "I know that when my hands start shaking, the Spirit is on me and God wants to do something good through my prayers."

"Do you think that everyone's hand shakes if the Spirit is on them?" I asked.

"No, but it has always been true with me. I don't know why. Maybe it is just God's way of letting me know He's with me."

During my last night at the house church, the members asked me to share my message on *The Five Love Languages*. Some of them had heard bits and pieces, and one of them had read my book. I focused on how understanding someone's primary love language will help more effectively meet the person's emotional need for love. I thought it would be helpful to them as they ministered to young people who so desperately needed love.

I did not anticipate Nicholas's response. As soon as I had finished, he rushed over and told me, "My love language is definitely physical touch, and now I know why my hand shakes when I pray. It's God's way of showing me that He loves me."

I put my arms around him, patted him on the back, and said, "He does indeed, and so do I." Tears came to his eyes and to mine.

PHYSICALLY CONNECTING WITH GOD

Wrestling with God

Evidence that God speaks the love language of physical touch is seen throughout the Bible—both Old Testament and New Testament. Genesis 32 records the account of Jacob on his way to returning to Esau, the brother from whom he had been estranged many years. Remembering how he had mistreated his brother and not knowing Esau's attitude after all that time, Jacob prayed. As he did, a man arrived and began to wrestle with him.

Perceiving the stranger to be a spiritual presence and messenger of God, Jacob held on to him and pleaded for a blessing. The mysterious figure did indeed bless Jacob, but first "touched the socket of Jacob's hip so that his hip was wrenched" as they wrestled. Jacob understood he was having an encounter with God as evidenced by his words, "I saw God face to face, and yet my life was spared."[2] The next morning Jacob was limping, which indicated that his experience was not simply a dream. He had been physically touched by God, and the event was a major turning point in his life.

Glowing from God's Presence

Moses also encountered God in a way that affected him physically. When he descended the mountain after God had given him the Ten Commandments, his face was radiant, although he didn't realize it. But it was clearly evident to other people—so much so that he had to place a veil over his face.[3]

Jesus' Public Ministry

The biblical account of the life of Jesus shows that He frequently used physical touch as a love language. As He taught in the villages, parents would bring little children to have Him touch them.[4] His disciples first rebuked the people, thinking that Jesus was too busy for children. But Jesus said, "I tell you the truth, anyone who will not receive the kingdom of God like a little child will never enter it." Then He took the children in His arms and blessed them.[5]

A number of Jesus' miracles involved physical touch as well. One man who had been blind from birth was asked how he had regained his sight. He replied, "The man they call Jesus made some mud and put it on my eyes. He told me to go to Siloam and wash. So I went and washed, and then I could see."[6] Two other blind men once asked for Jesus' help. That time He touched their eyes and their sight was restored.[7]

On other occasions Jesus went against all social protocol to touch "unclean" lepers, yet as He did, they were immediately cured of the disease. And one time when Peter's mother-in-law was sick with fever, Jesus touched her hand and the fever left her.[8]

Jesus also expressed the love language of touch to the twelve disciples. While Peter, James, and John were on a mountain with Jesus, His appearance underwent a stunning transformation. Three of the Gospels record this event, commonly referred to as the Transfiguration. This is Matthew's account:

> *His face shone like the sun, and his clothes became as white as the light. Just then there appeared before them Moses and Elijah, talking with Jesus.*
>
> *. . . A bright cloud enveloped them, and a voice from the cloud said, "This is my Son, whom I love; with him I am well pleased. Listen to him!"*
>
> *When the disciples heard this, they fell facedown to the ground, terrified. But Jesus came and touched them. "Get up," he said. "Don't be afraid." When they looked up, they saw no one except Jesus.*[9]

Washing the Disciples' Feet

One of Jesus' most profound instances of using physical touch to convey love took place during His last supper with the disciples. What makes this event so important is that the gospel account prefaced it with Jesus' intention:

> *Jesus knew that the time had come for him to leave this world and go to the Father. Having loved his own who were in the world, he now showed them the full extent of his love.*
>
> *The evening meal was being served, and the devil had already prompted Judas Iscariot, son of Simon, to betray Jesus. Jesus knew that the Father had put all things under his power, and that he had come from God and was returning to God; so he got up from the meal, took off his outer clothing, and wrapped a towel around his waist.*[10]

Jesus next filled a basin with water and began to wash His disciples' feet. He dried each man's feet with the towel. After He had finished, Jesus dressed once more and returned to His place. Then He explained His actions.

> *"Do you understand what I have done for you?" he asked them. "You call me 'Teacher' and 'Lord,' and rightly so, for that is what I am. Now that I, your Lord and Teacher, have washed your feet, you also should wash one another's feet. I have set you an example that you should do as I have done for you. . . . Now that you know these things, you will be blessed if you do them."*[11]

Here Jesus demonstrated two of the five love languages: acts of service and physical touch. It was common practice in Jesus' day that visiting guests would have their feet washed by the household servant.

Jesus took the role of the servant and lovingly washed the feet of His disciples. No doubt the touch of His hands was refreshing and restoring.

Followers of Jesus throughout the centuries have gone beyond mere words and used physical touch in their ministries. Someone once told Mother Teresa that he would not touch a leper for a million dollars. She replied, "Neither would I. If it were a case of money, I would not even do it for two million. On the other hand, I do it gladly for the love of God."[12]

The Ministry of the Apostles

After Jesus returned to His Father, God continued to work through the believers in the early church. They gladly carried on the serving, touching, and healing ministry of Jesus. For example, one day Peter and John were going up to the temple to pray. They encountered a man at the gate who had been crippled from birth who asked for money. Notice Peter's response:

> "Silver or gold I do not have, but what I have I give you. In the name of Jesus Christ of Nazareth, walk." Taking him by the right hand, he helped him up, and instantly the man's feet and ankles became strong. He jumped to his feet and began to walk. Then he went with them into the temple courts, walking and jumping, and praising God. When all the people saw him walking and praising God, they recognized him as the same man who used to sit begging at the temple gate called Beautiful, and they were filled with wonder and amazement at what had happened to him.[13]

The crippled man, after being touched by God through the hands of Peter and John, reciprocated his love by hugging the two apostles. An astonished crowd assembled, and Peter said, "Men of Israel, why does this surprise you? Why do you stare at us as if by our own power or godliness we have made this man walk? The God of Abraham, Isaac and Jacob, the God of our fathers, has glorified his servant Jesus." Peter described the death of Jesus ("the Holy and Righteous One") and explained that God had raised him from the dead. Then he added, "By faith in the name of Jesus, this man whom you see and know was made strong. It is Jesus' name and the faith that comes through him that has given this complete healing to him, as you can all see."[14]

PHYSICAL TOUCH WITH SPIRITUAL RESULTS

The language of physical touch demonstrated by Jesus and His followers did not end with a physical healing. The physical miracle was to validate Jesus' claims and convince people to respond to His love—to establish an eternal *spiritual* relationship with God. This is evidenced by what Peter said after the crippled man was healed. He urged his listeners, "Repent . . . and turn to God, so that your sins may be wiped out, that times of refreshing may come from the Lord, and that he may send the Christ, who has been appointed for you—even Jesus. He must remain in heaven until the time comes for God to restore everything."[15]

Peter was calling them to respond to the love of God. The touch of God, which brought healing to the blind, caused crippled men to walk, and delivered Nicholas from drug addiction, is always for the purpose of helping people make the God connection.

It has always been true that some people are skeptical when others claim to be "touched by God." But the greatest skeptics become the greatest believers when they personally experience God's touch. Saul of Tarsus is perhaps the best example. He was a first-century zealot intent on stamping out what he considered to be a heretical sect (Christianity) that claimed Jesus of Nazareth was the Messiah.

Saul was on his way to the town of Damascus with legal papers to arrest and return to Jerusalem anyone who was teaching this heresy. But as he neared Damascus, a bright light from heaven flashed around him. The dazed zealot fell to the ground. The book of Acts describes what happened next:

> [He] heard a voice say to him, "Saul, Saul, why do you persecute me?"
>
> "Who are you, Lord?" Saul asked.
>
> "I am Jesus, whom you are persecuting," he replied. "Now get up and go into the city, and you will be told what you must do."
>
> The men traveling with Saul stood there speechless; they heard the sound but did not see anyone. Saul got up from the ground, but when he opened his eyes he could see nothing. So they led him by the hand into Damascus. For three days he was blind, and did not eat or drink anything.[16]

Saul had been touched by God. Three days later God sent a man named Ananias to the house where Saul was staying. Significantly, Ananias placed his hands on Saul. Then he said, "Brother Saul, the Lord—Jesus, who appeared to you on the road as you were coming here—has sent me so that you may see again and be filled with the Holy Spirit." Something like scales immediately fell from Saul's eyes, and he could see again. Saul got up, was baptized, and got something to eat.[17]

He spent several days with the believers in Damascus and soon began to preach that Jesus is the Son of God. All who heard him were astonished not only at his message, but also at the complete change he had undergone.[18]

Saul was never the same. He would soon become known as the apostle Paul as he spent the rest of his life seeking to tell Jews and Gentiles about Jesus. He would be beaten, imprisoned, and often threatened by death, but nothing dampened the spirit of this man who had been touched by God.

Since the first century, thousands of men and women have been touched by God. They, in turn, have touched others as representatives of Christ. They work in hospitals, giving baths and wiping fevered brows. They are in rescue missions, kneeling beside the homeless with an arm draped around the shoulder of a needy person. They serve as "greeters" in their churches to smile, extend a hand, and give an affirming pat on the back as people enter the house of worship. They are channels of God's love, speaking fluently the love language of physical touch.

QUESTIONS FOR REFLECTION / DISCUSSION

(1) What would you say is the best example you've seen or experienced of receiving a "physical touch" from God?

(2) How might someone use physical touch appropriately to minister to:
- A visitor at church?
- A neighbor child playing in the yard?
- A homeless person on the street?
- An elderly person in a nursing facility?

(3) What other ways can you think of to "speak the love language of physical touch" in your worship of God?

Chapter Seven

DISCOVERING *Your Primary*
LOVE LANGUAGE

"How do I love thee? Let me count the ways."

When Elizabeth Barrett Browning asked and answered this question in her "Sonnet 42," she implied that the ways of expressing love are unlimited except by the human ability to be creative. Browning was right to an extent. When a man and woman are in the obsessive state of the "in love" experience, they can be extremely creative.

For example, Rhonda once told me about her husband's invitation to take the afternoon off and go flying with him. He was a farmer, so Rhonda was confused—but curious. Her husband had a pilot friend who took them up in his plane and flew over their farm. He tilted the plane a bit and Rhonda's husband pointed to the wheat fields below where she could read clearly the words, "I love you, Rhonda." Months earlier, the husband had carefully double-seeded those letters, knowing that once the wheat had sprouted, the words could be seen from the sky.

So Elizabeth Barrett Browning was right: People can be very creative. There are thousands of ways to express love.

However, most of us don't see that level of creativity very often in the course of daily life. Our expressions of love tend to fall into predictable patterns, and those patterns are greatly influenced by each person's primary love language. If your spouse's primary love language is words of affirmation and you speak that language often, your spouse will maintain a full love tank. If your own primary love language is acts of service, and your spouse speaks that language regularly, you will feel secure in his or her love. If, however, your spouse fails to communicate through acts of service and you fail to speak words of affirmation, neither of you will have a full love tank, even though you may use other love languages.

Couples can sincerely love one another yet not connect emotionally. The problem is not the lack of love; the problem is that they are not speaking each other's primary love language.

If I simply do what comes naturally for me, I will tend to speak my own love language. If my primary love language is words of affirmation, then I will tend to use words to express love for my wife. I am giving her what would make me feel extremely loved. Most of my creativity will be used in exploring various ways to verbally express my love for her. I may write love notes and leave them in unexpected places. I may request the local deejay to play her favorite love song on the radio. I may even write the words "I love you" in a wheat field. However, if her primary love language is not words of affirmation, words will not mean to her what they would mean to me.

RETURNING GOD'S LOVE IN OUR LANGUAGE

The same tendency is true when it comes to receiving and reciprocating God's love. Theoretically I may agree that God speaks His love to me in a thousand ways, but experientially I feel more deeply loved when I sense that God is speaking my primary love language.

One Monday morning I walked into my office and found that my secretary had placed a photocopy of a note from the offering plate the day before. It said simply:

To:
The church who shakes hands with me.
From:
Michael
Age: 5

No mention of the songs, sermon, drama, or stained glass windows. What church means to Michael is someone who shakes his hand. Michael's primary love language must be physical touch. I don't know if Michael has made the connection between God and God's helpers who attend his church, but I predict that soon he will. Someday God will shake Michael's hand and embrace him, and Michael will make the God connection.

Conversely, a person tends to express love for God in his or her primary love language. I first met Floyd in Houston. He was operating the sound system for a national convention of pro athletes. I had given my lecture on *The Five Love Languages* the day before. During one of our breaks, Floyd stopped me and said, "Your lecture on *The Five Love Languages* has helped me understand my marriage. My love language is physical touch, and my wife's love language is acts of service. To be honest, we have not been doing very well speaking each other's language. I never understood until now. I knew she complained that I didn't help her around the house. I also knew that she would often draw back when I tried to kiss or hug her. Now I understand; both of us have empty love tanks. I can't wait to get home and shock my wife by washing dishes, vacuuming the floors, and making beds. Do you think if I start speaking her language, she will start speaking mine?"

"I can't guarantee that," I said, "but I can tell you that's the best thing you can do to improve your marriage. If your wife begins to see that you are speaking her primary love language, there is a good possibility that she will begin to have warm emotional feelings for you and eventually will begin to reciprocate love."

Later, I had a more extended conversation with Floyd during which we discussed spiritual matters. I discovered that Floyd had become a follower of Jesus about three years earlier and was very active in a contemporary church. "I never cared much for God," he said, "and the church always turned me off. But a friend invited me to this new church. The place was wired. I felt God the first night I visited. The second time I went, I found myself overwhelmed by His presence. I was at the front of the church, weeping at the altar, before I knew what happened. That night I asked God to come into my life and forgive me of my past. It was the greatest night of my life."

I asked Floyd, "How do you express your love to God?"

"What I like is the praise music. I just reach out and touch God when I'm singing. I get goose bumps," he answered. "That's what moves me. It's like God is all over the place, and I am caught up in worshiping Him."

"It sounds like your love language toward God is also physical touch," I said.

Floyd was silent for a moment, then a smile broke across his face. "I've never thought of it that way, but you're right. It's when my emotions are moved and I feel the presence of God that my love tank fills up and I could worship God forever."

Floyd was confirming what I was coming to believe: that an individual's method of worship and of expressing love to God is strongly influenced by his or her primary love language. We can learn to speak other love languages, and we should; I'll discuss that later. But the most natural way for a person to experience and express love toward God is by speaking his or her primary love language.

THREE KEY QUESTIONS

How then do we discover our primary love language? In human relationships, I have often suggested the following approach. Ask yourself three questions.

(1) *How do I most often express love to other people?*

If you regularly express words of appreciation, affirmation, and love to others, there is a good chance that your primary love language is words of affirmation. You are giving to others what you would like to receive yourself. If you are often patting other people on the back, touching them on the shoulder, or giving appropriate hugs, then your primary love language may be physical touch.

(2) *What do I complain about most often?*

Your complaints reveal your inner emotional need for love. The wife who says, "We never spend time together anymore," is revealing that quality time is her primary love language. The husband whose primary love language is physical touch might say, "I just feel like you don't love me anymore. If I didn't initiate kissing you, I don't think you would ever kiss me." A daughter who complains, "You mean you didn't bring me anything from your trip?" is letting you know that she associates gifts with love.

(3) *What do I request most often?*

The wife who says, "Could we take a walk this evening after dinner?" is requesting quality time. If she *frequently* makes similar requests, she is revealing that her primary love language is quality time. We tend to request from others what would meet our deepest emotional need for love.

If you thoughtfully answer these three questions, you will likely discover your primary love language in human relationships. And once you discover your primary love language in human relationships, it is likely that the same will hold true for your relationship with God. However, if you want to confirm it, you can ask and answer the same three questions.

(1) *How do I most often express my love to God?*

If you are the kind of person who volunteers when the Bible study leader asks, "Who could make a meal to take to the Brown family?" you are demonstrating that your primary love language is acts of service. You genuinely feel that when you are serving others you are serving God. You are also deeply moved when you read about how Jesus healed the sick, fed the hungry, and washed the feet of His disciples. It is the serving nature of Christ that grips you most deeply and draws you to God.

Your neighbor's answer to that question may be altogether different. She may say, "I feel closest to God during my daily quiet time with Him. Every morning I get up early so we can spend time together. It's the highlight of my day. I sense that God is talking to me as I read the Scriptures, and I talk to Him as I pray. It's like a daily conversation with God—not unlike the way I talk with my husband when he comes home from work in the evenings." Such a response reflects that quality time is your neighbor's primary love language.

(2) *What do I most often complain to God about?*

Suppose you complain, "God, I feel like You have abandoned me. I don't feel close to You. I used to read Your Word and weep. Now I'm just reading words on a page. At church I used to feel Your presence when we sang, but now it seems like I'm just going through the motions. What's wrong?" This complaint is likely revealing that your primary love language is physical touch. It is what Floyd called the "manifest presence of God." He felt God's presence and sensed God's touch—not only spiritually, but also in his body.

On the other hand, perhaps you complain, "Lord, it seems like You're not blessing me anymore. For a while, every time I turned around You were blessing me. Now I can hardly pay the bills. It looks like I am going to lose my job, and our baby is sick. I don't understand." If that's your complaint, your primary love language probably is gifts. With job, money, and health, you felt loved by God. In their absence, you feel that God doesn't love you.

If someone complains that the pastor's sermons are rambling and meaningless, that person's primary love language probably is words of affirmation. If he or she does not hear anything meaningful from the pastor, the individual does not feel God's love through the sermon.

(3) *What do I request of God most often?*

Listen to the requests you make while praying, and you may discover your primary love language. Bob prays most often for wisdom, and acknowledges that his primary love language is words of affirmation. "As I read the wisdom literature of the Old Testament, particularly the book of Proverbs, I feel that I am walking close to the heart of God. Whenever the Holy Spirit shows me how to apply the wisdom of the Bible in my personal life, I feel that God is giving me personal attention, and I feel deeply loved."

Mary prays most often for the health of her children and that God will meet the financial needs of the family. She recognizes that receiving gifts is her primary love language. When God answers her prayers, she feels extremely loved by God.

Randall's most common prayer is, "Lord, I want to feel Your presence. I want to know Your power. I want to feel Your hand upon me. I want to be anointed by Your Spirit." When he experiences God's presence in a way that affects him physically and emotionally, he senses the love of God deeply and reciprocates with raised hands and flowing tears, and has even been known to dance in the presence of God. His love language is physical touch.

Doris's primary love language is quality time, and her most common prayer is, "Lord, my life is filled with activity and responsibilities, but more than anything, I want to spend time with You. Help me to find time." Her sister, Janice, has a much different prayer. "Lord, help me to find time to work in the soup kitchen. You know how much it means to me to serve others in Your name. Help me find time to do the ministry that is on my heart." Her primary love language is acts of service.

Most people will be able to identify their primary love language by answering the previous three questions. And a great many will also discover that their primary love language remains the same in both human relationships and their relationship with God.

WHY LEARN YOUR LOVE LANGUAGE?

The logical question is "How does understanding my primary love language affect my relationship with God and others?" Let me suggest the following ways.

(1) Better Self-understanding

Dave told me, "Nothing is more important in my life than the thirty minutes I spend with God every morning. I hear other people say that having a daily devotional time requires so much discipline on their part, but for me, it takes almost no discipline. I would rather have my devotional time than eat breakfast. It is where I find strength for the day. For me, it's a privilege to spend time listening to God and sharing my own thoughts and feelings with Him. It is what keeps my relationship with God alive."

Why is it so easy for Dave and so difficult for many others to maintain consistency in a daily quiet time with God? Because quality time is his primary love language and is the most natural and meaningful way of receiving and reciprocating the love of God.

Beth is a young single mother. After participating in a workshop I led called "The Love Languages of God," she said, "Now I understand why reading devotional books is so important to me. My love language is words of affirmation. Almost every morning when I read the comments of the writer, I find a sentence or an idea that speaks deeply to me and gives me the encouragement and strength and love to go on with my responsibilities. The words are like food to my soul. That's also why I have three or four CDs I play constantly in my car as I drive to work. I feel like I can conquer the world when I hear, 'He's my Rock and my Salvation; whom shall I fear?' I know that God is with me. The words of those songs give me the assurance that God loves me." Later in our conversation, Beth added, "Now I also understand why singing worship songs to God is so important to me. I feel like the words express my heart of gratitude and love to God better than anything else."

I met Roger at a church in Singapore. He was enthusiastic about his faith and told me about his weekly prayers with other men. "At our church we have a prayer meeting before the service. A small group of men gets together to pray for each other and for the service. One man gets on his knees while the other men lay their hands on his shoulders and pray for him. When the men place their hands on my shoulders and begin praying for me, it's like God has put His hand on me. It's the highlight of my week. I never feel closer to God than when those men are praying for me. I'm prepared not only for the service, but I'm ready to live another week loving God. Once in a while I have to miss the morning service because of my work, but I make sure I don't miss that weekly prayer meeting."

Knowing one's primary love language provides greater self-understanding. Someone else might find such a weekly prayer commitment uncomfortable and burdensome, but not Roger. Physical touch is his primary love language, and is how he feels the presence of God. When you know your primary love language, you understand why certain aspects of your relationship with God seem natural and speak so deeply to your soul.

(2) Better Ability to Understand and Help Fellow Believers

A second benefit of knowing your primary love language is to better understand fellow pilgrims who are different from you. This point became perfectly clear later during my conversation with Roger. He explained that his wife was critical of his desire to attend those weekly early-morning prayer meetings.

"She didn't understand how important it was to me until we discussed the love language concept, which also helped me understand her. In my heart, I was always critical of her because she didn't attend the women's prayer meeting. I thought she would go if she really loved God. But then I discovered that my wife's primary love language is quality time. She spends forty-five minutes every day in prayer and meditation over the Scriptures. I always felt guilty because I knew she was much better at that than I. Now I understand that the love she receives and gives to God in her daily time with Him is what I receive on Sunday mornings when God touches me. And she now understands how important my weekly prayer meetings are to me and my relationship with God."

Clearly, knowing someone's love language can help explain that person's walk with God—an especially important insight when the other person is one's spouse. Madeline was a cheerful woman whom I judged to be in her early fifties. She thanked me for helping her understand her husband, and told me her story.

"For years I complained about how much money he gives away. He gives to everybody who asks for money, even the men holding signs at the traffic light. I used to tell him, 'You're just giving them money to get drunk.' He would say, 'But maybe they're hungry.' He probably gives to seventy-five Christian organizations around the world. I don't mean just once; I mean every month. Our checkbook looks like a religious roster.

"Once I told him, 'If giving gets you to heaven, then you're going to have a mansion.' He replied, 'You don't get to heaven by giving. You get to heaven by accepting God's gift of eternal life through Jesus Christ. I'm not giving to get to heaven; I give because I'm going to heaven, and I want to show people the love of God on my way.'

"In my heart I knew he was right, but it always seemed to me that he was overdoing it. Now that I've heard about the five love languages, I understand him. Giving gifts is his primary love language. He is hopelessly in love with Jesus and his greatest joy is in giving to the causes of Christ around the world."

"Does he also give gifts to you?" I inquired.

"Oh, all the time!" she said. "I've never had any complaints about that, though sometimes I have felt he overdoes those also. But now I accept them and say thank you."

I asked, "So, do you give gifts to him as well?"

She said, "After we read and discussed your book, I realized I had not given him many gifts through the years and I asked if he had really felt my love. His response was, "Oh, Madeline, you have given me the gift of your presence, the gift of your commitment, the gift of your beauty, the gift of three children, the gift of hundreds of meals, the gift of encouragement.' He went on and on. To him everything is a gift."

"My guess is that your primary love language is not gifts," I continued.

"You're right," she said. "My love language is words of affirmation. And after we read the book he has become much better at speaking my language. Previously, he thought gifts were the answer to everything. Now he understands that we are different. He has always given me a fair amount of verbal affirmation, but now he is becoming proficient in speaking my language. However, the biggest difference is that I no longer complain about all that he gives away. I see that it is his way of loving God, and I am fortunate to be married to such a man."

Madeline's attitude changed when she understood her husband's primary love language.

"NOW I UNDERSTAND MY BROTHER-IN-LAW"

A few years ago, my wife and I were traveling on the Blue Ridge Parkway in the mountains of North Carolina. We stopped at a craft shop where she browsed while I occupied one of the rocking chairs on the front porch. The man beside me was friendly and began talking almost immediately. When he found out that I did counseling at a church, he said, "I've got a brother-in-law who goes to one of these Holy Roller churches. What do you think of those kinds of churches? Is that stuff real?"

Not wanting to answer before I fully understood the question, I inquired, "What kind of Holy Roller church is it?"

"Well, they say it is a Baptist church, but it's not like any Baptist church I've ever seen."

"Have you visited the church with your brother-in-law?" I asked.

"Once," he said, "and I swore I would never go back."

I asked him to describe it.

"Well, they sing these gospel songs and everybody gets happy and shouts. I mean, they run up and down the aisles and say, 'Hallelujah, praise the Lord.' One lady was waving a white handkerchief and crying, saying, 'Thank You, Jesus! Thank You, Jesus!' My brother-in-law raised both hands and danced in the aisle. It was like he was in a trance or something. It was like nothing I've ever seen."

"Have you talked with your brother-in-law about his religious beliefs?" I asked.

"Yes," he said. "Actually, we are both Baptists and agree on almost everything. He believes in the Bible; he believes Jesus is the Son of God and that we get to heaven by trusting in Jesus' death and resurrection. It's just that his worship style is so different from mine. To me, it's just too much emotion. I don't understand it."

By this time my wife had come out of the shop. I knew she wasn't interested in listening to me talk to a stranger for an hour about religion, so I told him, "I think I understand your brother-in-law but I don't have time to explain it." I went to my car, got a copy of *The Five Love Languages,* took it back to the man, and said, "Here's a book I wrote. It's not on the subject of religion. It's about marriage, but if you will read this book I think it will help you understand your brother-in-law."

I gave him my card and added, "After you've read the book, call me and we will discuss it further." He expressed appreciation for the book, and Karolyn and I continued our afternoon drive.

It was probably six months later when my secretary told me, "There's a man on the phone by the name of Horace; says he met you on the Blue Ridge Parkway." I didn't remember that he ever gave me his name, but I remembered the man, so I took the call. He began, "Do you remember our conversation on the Blue Ridge Parkway about my brother-in-law and his Holy Roller church?"

"I certainly do."

"Well, my wife and I read your book. How did you know that we were having trouble in our marriage?"

I laughed and said, "Well, I didn't, but I thought the book might help you understand your brother-in-law."

He said, "It did that, but it also helped our marriage. I don't read many books, but this one was easy to read and it made a lot of sense. My wife and I discussed it, and we are learning to speak each other's primary love language. It has really helped our relationship!"

I told him I was glad and then asked, "How about your brother-in-law? Did it give you any insight into him?"

"Well, the first thing I did after my wife finished reading the book was give it to my brother-in-law and his wife. They read it in a few weeks and discussed it with each other, and one night we had dinner together. He told us that his love language was physical touch and his wife's love language was acts of service. They had also been having some struggles in their marriage, and the book really helped them. I didn't make the connection right away, but the next week I was thinking about our conversation and why you would have given me a book on marriage when I was asking you a question about religion. Then it hit me. My brother-in-law's love language was physical touch, so his method of worship was physical.

"It was like a light came on, and I said to myself, *It stands to reason that his worship of God is physical because physical touch is his primary love language. When he raises his hands and dances in the aisle, he is really loving God.*

"A couple of weeks later I brought up the subject while my brother-in-law and I were hunting. He had not made the connection. But when I shared my thoughts, he said, 'You know, Horace, that makes a lot of sense. My wife is more of a quiet type and I always felt she was not as spiritual as I was because she did not get into worship like I did.

But now that I realize that her love language is acts of service, I see why she is always doing things for people. She fixes meals when somebody in the church is sick. When there is a death in the community, she goes over and helps clean the house for the family, and of course takes food. She visits in the nursing homes every week. Now I'm beginning to see this is her way of worshiping. She shows her love for God as she speaks her love language. Man, I'm glad we talked about this, Horace. I would never have thought about this if we hadn't had this conversation.'"

Horace concluded his "what happened after you left" account with a final suggestion. "So now I understand my brother-in-law and he understands his wife. Maybe you ought to write a book on the love languages of God. It might help a lot of people understand others better."

"Maybe I should," I said. "I'll give some thought to that."

I did give it some thought and this book is the result. I hope that many others will benefit from the insight that Horace experienced.

While Jesus was on earth, He prayed that those who became His followers would see themselves in unity not only with Him and His Father, but also with each other. In my opinion, one of the tragedies of the last two thousand years is that the followers of Jesus have been too often critical of each other. Some of the criticisms have focused on "methods of worship." Perhaps many of our differences can be reconciled as we understand that God uses various languages to speak to the human heart. As people respond to Him with different primary love languages, may His kingdom become strengthened rather than splintered.

QUESTIONS FOR REFLECTION / DISCUSSION

(1) By this point in this book, you probably already have a good idea of what your primary love language is. But answer the three questions to confirm and/or clarify your opinion:

- *How do I most often express love to other people?*
- *What do I complain about most often?*
- *What do I request most often?*

(2) As you answer the same three questions specifically in regard to your relationship with God, what discoveries do you make about the spiritual aspects of your life?

(3) Think about some of the disagreements or conflicts you've had with other believers based around methods of worship. After considering the different love languages and how they influence someone's relationship with God, can you better understand the other person's preferences?

Chapter Eight

LEARNING *to* SPEAK NEW DIALECTS *of* LOVE

We are creatures of habit. From the time we rise in the morning, we tend to go through the same routines day after day. Think about it. How different was this morning from yesterday morning? Chances are as you made your way from the bed to the bathroom your day began much as every day for months. The soap, the toothbrush, the washcloth, the toilet—they are typically approached in the same order.

Now, there is nothing wrong with order. In fact, doing the same things in the same order may even conserve time. But repetition may also foster dullness and, eventually, boredom.

People are innately creative. As we tap into our creative nature, life becomes more exciting and less predictable. For a number of years I have purposely chosen to vary my morning routine at least one day a week simply for the sake of variety. Maybe I have breakfast before shaving, rather than afterward. Perhaps I eat breakfast in suit and tie, rather than in my flannel pajamas draped over a V-neck T-shirt. I may even break my grapefruit/Cheerios routine and try something really radical, like white grape juice and Frosted Flakes. Some people have a routine of eggs, sausage, grits, and sawmill gravy, but for me that is about a once-a-year splurge!

I have enjoyed this bit of morning creativity so much that I have even begun to work it into the rest of my day. Nothing breaks the dullness of the afternoon like a twenty-minute drive to the other side of town to savor two Krispy Kreme doughnuts—with skim milk, of course. After such an outing, I can walk back into the office feeling like I have been on an adventure.

A growing number of employees are learning the value of such mini-vacations in the middle of the workday. Variety stimulates the mind and creativity livens up what could be a life of monotonous routine.

OPEN HEART, OPEN EYES

I would like to suggest that the same principle applies to a love relationship with God. If we only do what comes naturally and express love to God in our usual manner, it is possible that even a relationship with God will become routine.

Once while visiting England with my college-aged son, we spent an afternoon in Salisbury Cathedral. We walked together at first, but soon went our separate ways to linger before stained-glass windows, sit and observe sincere worshipers, marvel at the architectural style, and ascend the stairs to view the other side of the vaulted ceilings of the cathedral. As the sun began to set, Derek and I met outside on the grass of the beautiful lawn. Looking toward the cathedral, I asked him, "Would you like to pray?" He responded, "Dad, I have been praying for two hours."

I was silenced by his answer. Don't misunderstand me; I was deeply moved during the time I had spent in the cathedral. I had invited him to pray because I wanted us to share the afterglow of the experience. But I must be honest; it never occurred to me to pray as I walked through the cathedral. I was too absorbed in structure and form.

I realized that I tended to limit prayer to certain routine boundaries which I had established: sitting down or kneeling while closing my eyes and talking to God. My son had discovered a new dialect of prayer, one that involved walking—not only with an open heart but also with open eyes. He taught me a dialect I have enjoyed ever since. Now I often pray aloud as I drive down the freeway (with my eyes open, of course).

Each of the five love languages has many dialects, but many of us have limited ourselves to the few that come naturally to us. In this chapter, I want to explore the possibility of enhancing your love relationship with God by learning to speak new dialects of your primary love language. Or if you are really creative, you might try speaking a totally different love language, perhaps one you've never spoken before. If God is not limited in the love languages and dialects He speaks, we need not be, either. In true worship, we can learn to honor our Creator in many ways.

This chapter will reexamine each of the five love languages, and will add brief examples of various dialects within each language. These are only representative, of course. With a little creativity, you may discover a dialect that has never crossed your mind and, in so doing, bring a new dimension to your relationship with God.

WORDS OF AFFIRMATION
DIALECT #1: THANKSGIVING

One of the best-known dialects of words of affirmation is *thanksgiving*. Among my favorite psalms is Psalm 100, perhaps because I memorized it as a child. David wrote, "Enter [the Lord's] gates with thanksgiving" (verse 4).

Yet, even in this area, we tend to limit ourselves to the same specific expressions of thanks over and over again. "Thank You for my spouse and children. Thank You for our food. Thank You for life and health." When repeated often enough, such expressions may become simply routine and may even be spoken without conscious thought.

Giving Thanks for Things

Several years ago I was challenged to think more creatively about expressions of thanksgiving to God. Emily was attending a conference where I was speaking. I don't remember how the subject of thanksgiving worked its way into the conversation, but I do remember what she said. "Do you know how so much of our praying involves asking God for things? Well, I decided this week that I was not going to ask God for anything, but instead to thank Him for the things He had already given me. I looked around my house and realized that it was filled with things that made my life easier or brought back memories. So I determined to thank God for each of them."

Then Emily described how she did that. "I lay on my bed and thanked Him for it, mentioning the pillow, the mattress, the sheet, the blanket, and the beautifully decorated bedspread. I thanked Him for the phone and that it was cordless to enable me to walk around the house while I talked. I thanked Him for the nightstand and for the drawer that gave me a place to hide my neck brace. I touched the shade of the lamp on the nightstand and thanked Him for giving Thomas Edison such a wonderful idea and for letting me have a light to read by as I went to bed at night.

"I walked to the window, touched the blinds, and thanked Him that with a pull of one string I could have privacy. I touched the drapes and thanked Him that, not only did they match the spread, but several years earlier He had given me the ability to make them—which took my mind to the electric sewing machine. So I walked into the sewing room and thanked Him for the machine. While there, I thanked Him for the table on which I could stretch my fabric, for a yardstick, for patterns, and for a beautifully lighted room which stimulated my creative spirit.

"I walked to the bathroom, turned on the faucet, and thanked Him that I had running water. I touched the hot and cold faucets and thanked Him that I had a choice. I sat down on the commode and thanked Him that I did not have to walk a path to an outhouse like the one I had seen on my Uncle George's farm. I stepped into the shower and thanked Him that I didn't have to go to the river to take a bath. I thanked Him for the rugs that kept my feet from touching the cold tile floor and for the thick white towel that I wrapped around my body. When I looked at all the creams, oils, and tools sitting around my sink, I thanked Him not only for their presence, but for that voice within me that said as I looked in the mirror, 'Be creative; you can look better than that!'

"Later I sat in my chair in the den and thanked Him—not only for that chair but for all the chairs in my house. I walked through the room, touching every object. I touched the picture of my grandmother and thanked God for the reminder that I have a godly heritage. I touched the clock given to me by my grandfather just before he died and thanked God for his memory. I touched the two candles and thanked Him for a backup the next time a thunderstorm knocked out the electricity. I touched the books lying on the floor beside my chair and thanked Him for the many people who have enriched my life by their writings.

"For one hour," she said, "I walked through my house thanking God for the things He had given me. I still have four more rooms to go. I am going to have another hour of thanksgiving next week."

I have never forgotten my conversation with Emily. She enriched my life forever. Since then, I have established my own thanksgiving hours, touching most of the objects in my own house and verbalizing thanksgiving to God.

Giving Thanks for People

Of course, thanking God for material objects is but one small arena of thanksgiving. Another meaningful option is thanking God for the people He has brought into your life.

Try it sometime. You will be astounded at the number of people for whom you can give thanks. Start with your immediate family and move on to your extended family. (You may find yourself wanting to say about certain family members, "Thank You for this person, but I wish You had made him [or her] with a little more kindness." Don't yield to this temptation. Think of something good that the person has done or said and give God thanks.)

When you have acknowledged your extended family, think about the persons who taught you in school and in church. Dust off your school yearbooks, look through the pictures of your classmates, and thank God for all those whom you knew. Think about the people in your neighborhood who have done kind deeds through the years, friends in your Bible study group who continue to impact your life in a positive way, the people who stock the grocery shelves where you shop, the firemen and policemen who protect your city, and the sanitary engineer who collects your garbage each week. And be sure not to forget the people who have influenced your spiritual development through the years.

Giving Thanks for Nature and Your Unique Design

At another opportunity, spend time in thanksgiving for the natural world around you: grass and trees, flowers and butterflies, fleecy clouds and the winds that move them, raindrops on roses and sunshine on daisies, mountains and plains, beaches and rivers. During a visit to the zoo you can start your litany of thanksgiving for the world of animals.

Pull out the encyclopedia and do a little research on the human body. Thank God for your thyroid gland, sternum, stomach, and liver. Examine the various parts of the human brain, and thank God that those parts are functioning and that the whole thing is connected to your spinal cord. Observe the circulatory system and the cooperation between the skeletal and muscular system. Examine the digestive system, and thank God the next time you have a bowel movement. (Yes, really!) The human body will provide many hours of thanksgiving.

As you become more creative and reflective, you will "enter [God's] gates with thanksgiving." But thanksgiving is only one of the dialects of words of affirmation.

WORDS OF AFFIRMATION
DIALECT #2: PRAISE

The psalmist also challenged people in Psalm 100:4 to enter the Lord's courts with praise. Thanksgiving and praise are cousins. Praise focuses on who God is, while thanksgiving focuses on what God does.

In the Old Testament, the word for *praise* stems from the word *halal,* which is associated with making a noise. In fact, Psalm 100 begins with this command: "Make a joyful noise unto the Lord, all ye lands" (KJV). The Hebrew title for the book of Psalms is *Sepher Tehillim,* meaning Book of Praises.

Inner joy, which comes from making the God connection, is expressed in praise. Praise, therefore, is a mark of the people of God, and the whole of the Bible is punctuated with outbursts of praise. Conversely, nonbelievers are noted by their refusal to praise God.[1]

Verbal Praise

Praise to God may be expressed with or without music, in private, or in corporate worship with others. Verbal praise is a way of affirming our belief that God is holy, just, all-powerful, merciful, and loving. He is not only our Creator; He is also our Redeemer. He has made possible the love connection and, for that, we praise Him.

The realization that we are God's children now and forever should motivate us to praise Him. And if someone's primary love language is words of affirmation, it will be easy to express verbal praise to God. But again, it is easy to fall into the use of standard words and phrases, expressed at regular times and places. If this happens, even our praise, which starts out as authentic, can become mere ritual. Thus, we enhance our love relationship with God when we think creatively about places and ways to express praise to Him.

For example, stand in front of a window looking out on the beauty of God's creation and read aloud Psalm 19. Add your own words of praise as you go along. You may find yourself using terms of praise you have never used before.

Or get a Bible dictionary and look up the word "*God.*" As you read the article describing God's various characteristics, express your own words of praise for who He is.

Praise through Music

The singing of praises was central in both the Old Testament and the New Testament. The offering of praise is often associated with music. The book of Psalms, hymns, and praise choruses all can help stimulate your creativity as you look for words with which to praise God.

You need not be able to sing well in order to use these tools of praise. Pick up a hymnbook and sing one of the old hymns to God. Don't worry about staying on key. It does not matter to God whether or not you're a musician. (Remember that Psalm 100:1 said only to make a joyful *noise* unto the Lord!) After each stanza you sing, express your own words of praise to God.

One of the best ways to add dimension to your musical affirmations to God is to join others in expressing praise during *corporate worship*. Allow your heart to express itself to God through the words of the songs.

Much discussion has taken place about the increased popularity of so-called praise and worship music as opposed to the traditional hymns of the church. Is one musical form better than the other? Perhaps a lesson from history would provide some helpful perspective.

In 1692 Isaac Watts was an eighteen-year-old boy who refused to sing during the church services. One Sunday his father rebuked him for not singing. Isaac answered that the music was not worth singing because the psalms did not rhyme and were wooden and awkward in form and phrase. "Those hymns were good enough for your grandfather and father," said the senior Watts, "and they will have to be good enough for you."

But Isaac was insistent: "They will never do for me, Father, regardless of what you and your father thought of them."

"If you don't like the hymns we sing, then write better ones," his father said.

"I have written better ones, Father, and if you will relax and listen, I will read one to you." Isaac told his father he had been reflecting on the song of the angels in Revelation 5:6–10 and had rewritten it, giving it rhyme and rhythm:

"Behold the glories of the Lamb

Amidst His Father's throne;

Prepare new honors for His name

And songs before unknown."

His astonished father took Isaac's composition to the church. The congregation loved it so much that Isaac was asked to bring another the next Sunday, and the next, and the next, for over two hundred and twenty-two consecutive weeks.[2] Today Isaac Watts is considered the father of modern hymnody.

Three hundred years later, the young Isaac Wattses of our day are writing praise and worship music. The music expresses the rhythm and rhyme of their hearts. Those of us who have been accustomed to the hymns of Isaac Watts would do well to follow the example of Isaac's father and let the youth of our generation lead us into some fresh expressions of praise. In so doing, we may allow them to bless the church for the next three hundred years.

The dialects of praise are many because praise is not a matter of form; it is a matter of the heart. I suggest that you continue to use the dialects you have found meaningful in the past and then enhance your praise of God by trying new forms. Perhaps it is the desire to keep one's praise alive and heartfelt that explains why many young people who have been raised with informal, free-flowing styles of worship are now finding themselves attracted to more liturgical worship. The reading of liturgies, which may have become ritual to someone who has repeated them for thirty years, can be like fresh water to a young person who has never heard them.

My plea is that believers will cease from criticizing styles and forms that are not familiar to them. Instead, let us seek to keep our own praise genuine by searching for ways new to us, but known and understood by the God whom we seek to praise.

WORDS OF AFFIRMATION
OTHER DIALECTS

I have discussed only two basic dialects pertaining to the words of affirmation love language. There are many more.

You might try writing God a love letter. (Yes, you may use your computer.) After all, He has written you several letters. (Twenty-one books of the New Testament are letters that were written through the apostles, yet are divinely inspired.) Why not read a chapter of Scripture to determine what is on God's heart, and then write a letter expressing your response?

If you are poetic, you can write a poem. If you are musical, you can even express your affirmation in a song. If you are a vocalist, you can sing it to God and to others. (If you are not a vocalist, sing it to God alone.)

The dialects for expressing love to God through words of affirmation are limitless. You may learn of new dialects by reading the writings of others who have this primary love language, from friends in a discussion group, or on your own during moments of quiet meditation. Ask the great Creator to touch the spirit of creativity within you, and you may discover dialects of words of affirmation that had never crossed your mind.

QUALITY TIME
DIALECT #1: PRINTED RESOURCES

If your primary love language is quality time, then you will deeply anticipate those moments when you can have time alone with God. You can easily identify with Karen, who said, "The highlight of my day is my 'quiet time' with God."

When I inquired about what she did during her "quiet time" with God, she replied, "Usually I read a chapter in the Bible, underline key phrases or words, then talk to God about those words or phrases. Sometimes I ask God questions. Sometimes I express gratitude. Other times I confess my sins that were revealed as I read the chapter. Then I typically read a commentary to see what other people have thought as they read the chapter. I am often affirmed to see that others were touched by the same idea that gripped my own mind, and I sometimes find answers to my questions."

Karen would follow her commentary reading with the daily selection in one of her devotional books. "I respond to God about what I read in the devotional," she told me. "Then I have an extended prayer time in which I lay my day, my family, and my concerns before Him to ask for His wisdom and guidance. I sometimes end by singing a song to God. I am not much of a musician, but I think God hears the melody of my heart.

"I talk to God periodically throughout the day," Karen continued, "but my morning quiet time is what sustains my spirit. It prepares me to face the day. I often compare it to my marriage. When Jim and I have our daily 'couple time' where we share our lives with each other, I feel connected to him and our marriage seems healthy. When, for whatever reason, we fail to have those quality times together, I feel distant. My quiet time with God is what gives me the sense of being close, or intimate, with God."

"Where and when do you spend this quality time with God?" I inquired.

"The only time that really works for me is in the morning before my family wakes up," she said. "My place is in the basement at a little table in the corner of the laundry room. Aesthetically, it does not have much to offer, but for me it is a cathedral. Sometimes, as I leave the room I start a load of laundry and look at my sign above the washer: 'Remember, you are washing clothes for Jesus.' I discovered that truth during my quiet time with God, from Colossians chapter 3," she said, paraphrasing verse 17.

Perhaps you can identify with Karen. If your primary love language is quality time, you may also have a time, a place, and a method of spending quality time with God. But if you have not yet established a regular quiet time, you may find Karen's description extremely attractive. For her the love language of quality time is the deepest expression of her love for God, and she most keenly senses His love for her by using various printed resources during her daily interactions with Him.

QUALITY TIME
DIALECT #2: WALKING WITH GOD (LITERALLY)

However, there are numerous other dialects of quality time. Patrick's love language is also quality time, but his personality does not lend itself to the pattern described by Karen. He is a man on the move who likes to walk as much as Karen enjoys sitting and meditating.

When I asked Patrick how he spent quality time with God, without hesitation he said, "Oh, God and I have wonderful walks together during which I memorize verses of Scripture. A friend once shared the idea with me, and I have been doing it for several years. I print the verse on the back of one of my business cards. My friend gave me a little leather packet for storing the verse cards. I carry them with me when I walk, and I review the verses, talking to God about each one. Some verses lead me to confess a sin. Other times I am motivated to cry out for God's help to apply the principle of the verse to my life. Some stimulate me to pray for other people."

Patrick's method of spending quality time with God is clearly quite different from Karen's method, but they are simply different dialects of the same love language. Both people spend quality time in conversation with God.

QUALITY TIME
DIALECT #3: REGULAR EXTENDED TIME WITH GOD

Julia described yet a third dialect of quality time. "My life is so hectic with raising three children, working a full-time job, and trying to be a wife to Rob. The idea of a daily quiet time with God is intriguing to me, but I have never been able to make it work. So what I have done is carve out one three-hour period each week during which I have extended time with God. Usually it is Thursday morning from 9:00 to 12:00. Thursday is the lightest day in my workweek, and my employer has agreed to give me those three hours off each week—without pay, of course.

"That period of time is the highlight of my week. I don't know what I would do if I did not take that extended time to get alone with God. In the summer I go to the city park. There are several picnic tables, and I can always find one that is empty. In the winter I go home. The kids are in school, my husband is at work, and the house is quiet, so I turn our living room into a worship center."

At home Julia sings hymns, reads Scripture, and often reads biographies. Reading about the lives of others encourages her, she reports.

"As I sing and read, I talk to God. I express my worship to Him and I ask for His help and guidance in my life. Sometimes I am tempted to do housework during those three hours," Julia confessed. "But I have not yielded to that temptation. To do so would defeat the whole purpose of spending quality time with God. Someday I hope to be able to have a daily quiet time, but for now this is what works for me. Without it, I am not sure that I would survive the pressures of life. What really encourages me is that I believe God is as excited about our time together as I am. I would feel like I was letting Him down if I did not show up."

Obviously, Julia has learned to speak a dialect of quality time that is meaningful to her and enhances her relationship with God.

QUALITY TIME
DIALECT #4: BEGINNING AND ENDING
THE DAY WITH GOD

Robert was a manufacturer's representative for several companies who traveled extensively. I knew him to be a devoted follower of Jesus, and I also knew that his primary love language was quality time. I asked him, "How do you find time to develop your relationship with God when you are on the road so often?"

"No problem," he said. "Every morning before I leave the hotel room, I spend ten minutes listening and talking to God. I carry a little devotional book in my briefcase. I always read the verse for the day and the comments, and then I talk to God about what I have read and ask for His guidance.

"When the day is over, I am usually in another city, often having dinner with customers. If the weather is nice when dinner is over, I find a public park and take a walk with God, praying about the day, about my family, and about missionaries who are friends of mine. After the walk I sit down and read a chapter in the Bible, underlining the things that seem most important to me and talking with God about them. If the weather is inclement, I use the hotel fitness center for some exercise and read the Bible in my room.

"Beginning and ending my day consciously talking to God keeps me close to Him. I have been doing this for many years, and I cannot imagine not spending time with God every day. In many ways, those are the most important parts of my day. And after I finish reading the Bible, I call my wife and catch up on what has happened at home. So we have our quality time on the telephone."

QUALITY TIME
OTHER DIALECTS

I have cited four examples of different dialects of the love language quality time, but there are many more. If your primary love language is quality time and you genuinely love God, you will find a way to have quality conversations with Him that fits your lifestyle. Variety in time, place, and method may well enhance your expressions of love to God.

For example, if a cathedral or church is nearby, you might arrange to have your quality time with God in this setting.

If you are an indoor person, you might try having quality time with God outdoors, even in challenging weather. Talking to God in the rain can be a rewarding experience if you acknowledge that He is the God who sends the rain.

If your schedule is filled, then skipping lunch and using the time to be alone with God may be more filling than the best steak you have ever tasted. Finding a time and a place may be difficult in our fast-paced world, but the heart that longs for God will make time for Him. People with the love language of quality time reflect the attitude of the psalmist: "As the deer pants for streams of water, so my soul pants for you, O God. My soul thirsts for God, for the living God. When can I go and meet with God?"[3]

It is the intense longing of the heart that leads us to be creative in speaking to God during periods of quality time. And even if quality time is not your primary love language, you may be inspired by some of these stories and determine to learn this language by speaking one of the various dialects . . . or coming up with one of your own.

GIFTS
DIALECT #1: MONEY

Expressing one's love to God through gifts is not limited to money.

However, monetary gifts are common and are a logical starting point as a dialect for the love language of gift giving.

A young couple who had been married only six months once accepted my challenge to give a thousand dollars to our church's annual missions offering by the end of one year. The plan I suggested was simple: Make the decision and then put aside twenty dollars each week for fifty weeks.

One year later the couple visited my office with an envelope containing fifty twenty-dollar bills; they planned to put it in the offering plate the next Sunday. They were elated at the joy of giving to God's work around the world.

The wife said, "A couple of times we discussed using some of this money for personal needs, but then we both would shake our heads and say, 'No, that is our gift to God. We dare not use it for ourselves.'"

A week or two later, I visited Jan and Mike, a couple I have known for many years. I had been invited to speak at their church and was still excited about the annual missions offering at my own church, especially the example set by the newlyweds. After hearing about the younger couple, Mike offered to tell me his and Jan's story.

"Jan and I had both been taught to give 10 percent of our income to God, so that's what we agreed to do as a couple. At the end of our first year of marriage, I told her, 'You know, in the Old Testament people gave a tenth of their income, but we who have been blessed with the gift of eternal life through Jesus and have the Holy Spirit who gives us power should really give more.' I asked Jan what she would think about our increasing our giving to 11 percent, instead of 10. She agreed, and at the end of the year we had more money left over than we had the year before. Since God had blessed us so much, we decided to increase our giving to 12 percent. It became a pattern of life. Every year we had more left than the previous year, so every year we raised our giving by 1 percent."

"How long have you been married?" I asked.

With a smile he said, "Forty-nine years."

It did not take me long to do the math and realize that he and his wife are now giving 58 percent of their income to God. I could tell their giving was a source of nothing but sheer joy for the two of them.

GIFTS
DIALECT #2: MEETING PHYSICAL NEEDS OF OTHERS

Yet rather than setting aside money, some people with the love language of gifts prefer to stay attuned to the immediate needs of those around them. Jesus suggested that a cup of cold water given to a thirsty person is an expression of love to God that will not go unnoticed by the Father.[4]

Loving God is often expressed by meeting the physical needs of other people: food, drink, clothing, and shelter. Nothing delights some givers more than to be the channel of meeting the physical needs of others. When the local Boy Scout troop makes its annual plea for food for the needy, those people are among the first to respond. When a local radio station calls for contributions to help those who live in flooded areas, they are the first to respond with clothing and other items.

However, I have a friend whose primary love language is gift giving, but he seldom responds to those kinds of pleas. He is an investor who regularly gives his most profitable stocks to Christian organizations, and nothing makes him happier. He is able to avoid paying capital gains taxes by donating stocks, and at the same time he benefits Christian endeavors worldwide. He takes great delight in this double-edged gift giving.

GIFTS
DIALECT #3: GIVING ENCOURAGEMENT

Another dialect of gift giving requires no money or wealth at all, yet still speaks deeply of one's love for God. It is the gift of encouraging words.

Jim lives in a small textile-mill village in a house more than seventy years old and in need of repair. He is an exuberant follower of Jesus with empty coffers but a full heart and a desire to give to others.

"I wasted the first fifty years of my life," he said. "I allowed alcohol and drugs to control me. But one night at a rescue mission I turned my life over to Christ, and the leaders of the mission invited me to live on a farm that they operated. During the year I spent on the farm I realized that I did not have to be controlled by alcohol and drugs, but that the Spirit of God wanted to make something good out of my life.

"The last fifteen years of my life have been the best. I have had a steady job. I am buying my own house, and best of all, I have a family of friends at my church who love me. I don't have large sums of money to give to the church, but my friends tell me that does not matter. What I do give is words of encouragement. I think of the verses of Scripture that helped me turn my life around, write them out on cards, and give the cards to people when I feel it is appropriate. Many people have told me how much the verses have meant to them. I also pray with people. Prayer is a great way to encourage others."

Jim is expressing his love to God by giving gifts, and he doesn't have to spend a nickel to do so.

GIFTS
OTHER DIALECTS

I have another friend who gives regularly to his church, but what really excites him is giving to a particular project. For example, when

Joni Eareckson Tada's "Wheels for the World" came to his attention, he responded by giving fifteen wheelchairs, and that is just one of the many projects to which he has given through the years. For him, envisioning a specific gift for a specific purpose makes his giving a greater expression of love to God. He speaks a dialect of gift giving with which many people can identify.

Let me suggest that if gift giving is your primary love language, you consider learning new dialects of giving. Expand your horizon by giving in different ways. For those who usually give money, consider food. For those who regularly give tangible items, consider nonmaterial gifts, such as words of encouragement. With a little creativity, you can expand your primary love language and learn new dialects that will enhance your expressions of love to God. On the other hand, if giving has always been hard for you, consider trying any of the previous dialects in an effort to learn the love language of gift giving.

ACTS OF SERVICE
DIALECT #1: USING RETIREMENT FOR GOD

People whose primary love language is acts of service use whatever skills they have to do the work of God. They are following the example of their leader, Jesus, of whom it was said, "He went around doing good."[5] They are not all technically skilled, but receive great satisfaction from helping others by raking leaves, cleaning gutters, removing snow, delivering meals, and limitless other ways. They reach out to serve others as an expression of their love for God.

Carl retired twenty years ago from his job as an electrical engineer. Since then, he has built bunk beds at a youth camp in Honduras, a new dining hall and kitchen for a seminary in the Philippines, and three new homes for missionaries in West Africa. He has also remodeled dorms and kitchens at a youth camp in Peru, helped build display cases for a bookstore in Honduras, and helped build a base camp for international mission volunteers in Albania.

Why is a "retired" engineer still at work? Because Carl loves God and his primary love language is acts of service. In addition to his work in other countries, he has devoted one year to supervise the building of a sanctuary for a new church in Georgia and another year to do the same for a church in North Carolina. He has built bookcases for the pastor of a small church in New Jersey, helped remodel classrooms for an academy in Tennessee, and teaches a Bible class in his own church when he isn't on missions trips.

Carl has only one regret: "I'm sorry I didn't retire sooner so I could have done more."

ACTS OF SERVICE
DIALECT #2: COOKING

As long as I have known Marie, her stove has seldom been cold. Her kitchen is her place of worship as she demonstrates her love for God by preparing food for others. When her husband shows up at my door with a meal from Marie, I am reminded of her devotion to God. When I am out of town on speaking engagements, my wife has an open invitation to stop by Marie's for some mint tea, fellowship, and whatever goodies happen to be coming out of her oven that day. Recently, Marie provided a meal for her entire Bible fellowship group—forty-six people.

For Marie, such feeding projects are not a burden. They are her delight. It is her way of loving God.

ACTS OF SERVICE
DIALECT #3: BUILDING

My friend Mark never cooked a meal in his life, but he speaks the acts of service love language just as fluently as Marie. Mark works for the airline industry, but every Christmas and Easter season you will find him on a scaffold high above his church's choir loft building sets for the holiday presentations. For two weeks he oversees volunteers and turns them into professional builders. His finished sets would rival Broadway's. He is not motivated by money or praise from others. He much prefers to stay in the background and express his love to God by building stage sets. Yet, thousands of people are blessed each Christmas and Easter because Mark speaks the love language called acts of service.

When it comes to builders, perhaps none is more prolific than Millard Fuller, founder of Habitat for Humanity. He is a tall and slender man with the enthusiasm of a winning football coach. The first time I met him I was among a group of volunteers who felt we were about to embark upon the greatest adventure of our lifetime. One week later, when the house was totally finished, we gathered for the dedication and presentation of the house to the new owner.

As Millard made the presentation, he handed the owners a Bible along with the keys to the house. He read the inscription for all to hear: "Jesus did many other miraculous signs in the presence of his disciples, which are not recorded in this book. But these are written that you may believe that Jesus is the Christ, the Son of God, and that by believing you may have life in his name."[6] He explained that his motivation for founding Habitat for Humanity was to show the love of God, and his prayer was that all people would come to know Jesus Christ in a personal way. I knew that he was not simply a social do-gooder. He was a man deeply in love with God. Habitat for Humanity was a distinct dialect for speaking his love language.

ACTS OF SERVICE
OTHER DIALECTS

The dialects of acts of service are essentially endless. I still think of James, one of the deacons while I was pastor of a small church in North Carolina over forty years ago. He was an electrician by trade, but he was also a skilled plumber. He pulled me aside one day and said, "Now, preacher, when your house or the church needs any plumbing or electrical work, don't you call a plumber or electrician; you call me. I can't do much for the Lord, but I can do plumbing and electrical work. That's my way of saying thank You to God for all He has done for me. You hear?" I heard, and every time I needed James's help it was a joy to watch him demonstrate his love for God.

Recently, while in the grocery store, I encountered a mother and her three children, ages eight, ten, and twelve. I had counseled with her and her husband several years earlier, so I knew that her primary love language was acts of service. When I asked, "What are you and the children doing this summer?" she replied, "One day a week we all go downtown to the local soup kitchen and help serve lunch and clean up afterwards. The children love it." It was encouraging (but not surprising) to see her expressing her love to God in such a manner. It was also heartening to see that she was teaching her children to speak this love language. Most of the mothers I meet in the summer are taking their children to the swimming pool or to a sports event. How refreshing to see a mother teaching her children to love God by loving others.

If acts of service is not your primary love language, let me encourage you to find a simple project and expand your vocabulary in learning to love God by serving others. And if it *is* your primary love language, my challenge for you is to learn new dialects and enhance your love relationship with God. Keep in mind the many worthwhile programs such as Meals on Wheels (which involves taking meals to the elderly and sick). Or try being a teacher's aide, going on a missions trip, or volunteering at your local church or hospital. Your opportunities are limited only by your willingness to explore.

PHYSICAL TOUCH
DIALECT #1: TOUCHING THE "UNTOUCHABLES"

Every society has a segment of *untouchable* people. In first-century Palestine, they were the lepers and prostitutes. The lepers lived apart from the rest of the population and were compelled to cry aloud "Unclean! Unclean!" when another person approached. The prostitutes were so abhorred that the religious leaders concluded that Jesus could not be a prophet and allow such a woman to "wet his feet with her tears . . . [wipe] them with her hair, [kiss] them and [pour] perfume on them."[7]

In Western society we also have our untouchables. By our behavior we demonstrate that certain people are to be avoided. The categories differ from individual to individual, but include people with AIDS, "street people," sex offenders, the mentally incompetent, the physically grotesque, and the spiritually cultish. But the love of God cuts across all such barriers. Those who truly love Him will be His agents for touching the untouchables.

My friend Joe Stowell, president of Cornerstone University, told me about Lisa. At age seventeen she had gone to Los Angeles on a short-term missions trip where she became burdened for prostitutes. Sensing God's call on her life to help such women whom most of society would rather not think about, she enrolled at Moody Bible Institute in Chicago, where Joe was then president, and majored in urban ministries. After graduation she began to search for an organization that ministered to prostitutes, but no such ministry existed. So Lisa started Salvage House. Every night from 9 PM until 1 AM, she and a teammate walked the streets of Chicago looking for prostitutes open to positive change in their lives. (Two male team members accompanied them for protection.) Lisa's approach was simple: Build relationships and provide a place where the women could find physical safety and (if desired) spiritual guidance. In Lisa's Salvage House, women for whom physical touch had been a means of exploitation discovered the warm embrace of truly loving arms. For several years now, the caring touch of Lisa and her teammates has helped many women experience the love of God.

We tend to underestimate the importance of touch . . . especially to those who don't regularly receive it. I was talking to a long-term friend whom I had not seen for some time and asked what he was doing during the summer. He told me, "Bobby [his son] and I have been going to the rescue mission every Monday night. We shake hands with all the men as they come into the mission; we pat them on the back and hug them; we bow on our knees and place our arms on the shoulders of those who come for prayer at the end of the service. Some of my friends say they can't believe that we are doing this, but for Bobby and me it's the most exciting part of our summer. I know that most of those men do not get many handshakes, hugs, and pats on the back. I feel like we are being God's representatives to show His love to them."

It is often the fear of disease that keeps people from touching the untouchables. I asked Bobby's father about his concerns for their physical health. He said, "We try to take normal precautions. We wash our hands before we go to the rescue mission. We are careful not to put our hands near our noses or mouths. We wash our clothes and take a shower as soon as we get home. So far we haven't had any problems."

All too often I hear, "I don't want to get close to AIDS patients. I'm afraid I'll get it." Learning and following good health habits is extremely important, particularly for those who work among people who have communicable diseases. I'm not suggesting that in our efforts to love others we minimize potential dangers. But no one contracts AIDS by giving a hug to someone with the disease. And we must never allow ungrounded fear to keep us from expressing love to God by making physical contact with His people who live on the edges of society.

PHYSICAL TOUCH
DIALECT #2: MINISTRY IN INSTITUTIONAL SETTINGS

Mary and her thirteen-year-old daughter speak the language of physical touch. They go once a week to an assisted living complex for aging adults. When I asked what they did there, she said, "Mostly we just love them." I pressed for more details, and she continued, "I think one of the most important things we do is touch those people. It's amazing how many of them extend their hand when we walk by. They're eager for a handshake. When we get ready to leave the room after our visit, those who are able often stand up and reach out for a hug. Of course, whether they reach out or not, I hug them. You know me; I'm a hugger." For Mary, hugging is a way of expressing love.

People who live in institutional settings such as nursing homes, prisons, and extended-stay hospitals often are deprived of loving, physical touches. Some do not have family members who visit, and those who do may have relatives who are not "touchers." Therefore they are extremely open to anyone who will express love to them through physical touch. Mary confirmed, "I have never had anyone turn away from me or draw back from my hugging them. I get the feeling that they look forward to our coming because they know they are going to get a hug."

PHYSICAL TOUCH
OTHER DIALECTS

While Mary and her daughter found the value of hugs in an institutional setting, the power of a hug can be appreciated in almost any setting, although there are exceptions. Karolyn and I were having dinner out one night with our friends King Brown and his wife, Frances. King was eighty-two years old and was still wearing the same badge I've seen him wear for thirty years. It read, "Hugging is a contact sport."

In the midst of our dinner conversation, a long-time acquaintance of Karolyn's and mine came over to say hello. I proceeded to introduce her to King and Frances, at which time King stood up and reached out to hug her. Her response was immediate and unexpected. She stepped back and said, "The only man I allow to hug me is my husband."

King was clearly surprised, but sat down and said, "I can appreciate that." My friend proceeded to explain her rationale, and he again acknowledged her opinion. But when she left, King told us, "In over sixty years of hugging, she's the second person who has ever refused a hug. I guess two in sixty years is not so bad."

I have never known anyone who speaks the love language of physical touch more fluently than King. As we left the restaurant, I was encouraged to see the way he helped Frances get her coat on, patted her on the back, and held her hand as they walked to the car. After five children and fifty years of marriage, he still expresses his love by affectionate touch.

His chief dialect of physical touch is hugging people. Young or old, male or female, married or single, anyone who encounters him will be hugged. King once told me, "You'd be surprised how many people tell me that my hug is the first hug they've had in a month. I don't think people realize how powerful it is to give a hug." And if someone engages him in conversation, in less than five minutes he will be talking about God. As long as I have known him, King has been passionately in love with God.

When we understand that people are made in the image of God, that God loves them intensely, and that we are His representatives on the earth, physical touch becomes more than a social grace. It becomes a meaningful expression of God's love.

Jim also combines physical touch with spiritual care for others. He feels that praying for people is the most powerful thing someone can do. If you share a prayer request with him, he doesn't write it on a sheet of paper to be prayed for later. He says, "Let's pray about that now." And when he prays for someone, he always makes physical contact with the person—perhaps extending a hand or placing his hand on the other's shoulder.

His prayers are simple but intense. When he finishes praying, he typically gives the person a pat on the back and an embrace. One man told me, "When Jim puts his arm on my shoulder and prays for me, I feel like God has placed His arm on my shoulder and is listening intently to what Jim is saying." For some people, Jim's physical touch is the touch of God.

Before leaving the topic of physical touch, it should be noted that some people have become leery of this love language because touch has been misused in contemporary culture—often to the point of exploitation of other people. I am compelled to clarify that true expressions of love via physical touch should always be for the benefit of the person touched. As soon as the motive becomes to manipulate or satisfy one's own sensual desires, physical touch ceases to be an expression of love— much less God's love. However, those with pure intentions must not allow the fear of being misinterpreted to keep them from speaking the authentic love language of physical touch.

A friend of mine recently returned from Kenya and described a conversation with a woman whose husband had become a Christian. He had asked her, "What is the greatest change you noticed when your husband became a follower of Jesus?" She responded without hesitation, "He stopped beating me." Those who are true followers of Jesus will never use physical touch as a means of harming others, but will view it as a vehicle of expressing God's love.

The purpose of this chapter is to encourage you to enhance your love relationship with God by using new dialects of your primary love language. And perhaps you will be inspired to explore the possibility of learning to speak a second or third love language to God. It is my hope that in speaking new languages and dialects, your love relationship with God will continue to grow and be forever vibrant.

QUESTIONS FOR REFLECTION / DISCUSSION

(1) Consider your natural inclinations, experience, and preferences, and list the five love languages in an approximate order. Begin with your primary love language and end with the one that is most unlike you.

Words of Affirmation
Quality Time
Gifts
Acts of Service
Physical Touch

(2) For each of the love languages, determine at least one dialect that you would be willing to do if the opportunity came along to use that action as an expression of love to God.

Words of Affirmation—

Quality Time—

Gifts—

Acts of Service—

Physical Touch—

(3) What opportunities might you have this week to do some of the things you have listed? If you fail to think of any such opportunities, ask God to direct you to people who will benefit from receiving His love through the exercise of your love language(s).

Chapter Nine

LOVE LANGUAGES
and GOD'S
DISCIPLINE

Real love includes discipline. With genuine love comes the desire to correct the errant behavior of those close to us. When psychiatrist Ross Campbell and I wrote *The Five Love Languages of Children,* we included a chapter on love and discipline, noting that truly loving parents will by necessity provide discipline for the child. Helping children learn to operate within parameters is an essential part of preparing them to live as responsible citizens in an adult world.

Ross and I made two key observations. First, a child is most likely to rebel against discipline when his or her emotional love tank is empty. We encouraged parents to speak the child's primary love language before and after any disciplinary action. Second, we observed that the child is most sensitive to the method of discipline that is related to his or her primary love language. If, for example, the child's primary love language is words of affirmation, then words that point out the child's improper behavior will be felt very strongly. While a child is experiencing such discipline, he may feel estranged from the parents and even conclude that the parents do not love him or her.[1]

The child's difficulty in understanding parental discipline often becomes the adult's struggle to properly comprehend the discipline of God. The same two principles seem to hold true. First, *we are most likely to rebel against the discipline of God when our spiritual love tanks are empty.* If we do not feel God's love, then His discipline may seem excessively harsh. Second, *when God's method of discipline relates directly to our primary love language, it strikes us at the deepest possible level.*

GOD'S LOVING DISCIPLINE

Many people have a limited, if not completely erroneous, definition of "discipline." Some equate the word with punishment. But as I refer to discipline throughout this chapter—especially the discipline of God—I do not necessarily mean punishment for bad behavior. In the same way that we might choose to discipline ourselves by not eating during a diet, or to discipline ourselves through an exercise regimen to get in better shape, parents sometimes discipline their children with the goal of making them stronger or more well-rounded. And God will frequently discipline His children—always in love—to become more the people they were created to be, thereby making their lives more complete and satisfying.

One reason discipline is so frequently associated with punishment is because we neglect to voluntarily enforce disciplines soon enough. Parents may not see their children's need for discipline until the children are distancing themselves from the parents and falling in danger of bringing harm to themselves or others. Similarly, the longer adults are walking apart from God, the less likely they are to feel His love. A sense of "distance" develops. Yet when God reaches out to lovingly discipline them, they often interpret His methods as being severe.

We may accuse God of being unfair, but in reality it is our movement away from Him that creates the "distance." When we remain in intimate fellowship with God, His discipline is much more likely to be interpreted as an act of love rather than judgment.

Since we are by nature most sensitive to the discipline that relates directly to our primary love language, God often chooses that language to bring us to a place of repentance and forgiveness. When we are on a destructive pathway and God really wants to get our attention, He often disciplines us in keeping with our primary love language. For example, for people who respond best to words of affirmation, the heavens become silent. Work colleagues begin to deliver messages of condemnation. Spouses and children become critical. Even during Bible readings, such people are drawn to the passages that reveal sinfulness and are aware that those portions of Scripture are the words of God to them. With empty hearts, they cry out to God in desperation and begin their journey homeward.

God knows us better than we know ourselves. He knows how to get our attention. His discipline is not always pleasant, but it is always purposeful. The author of the New Testament book of Hebrews makes this point clearly:

> *"My son, do not make light of the Lord's discipline, and do not lose heart when he rebukes you, because the Lord disciplines those he loves, and he punishes everyone he accepts as a son."*
>
> *Endure hardship as discipline; God is treating you as sons. For what son is not disciplined by his father?... Our fathers disciplined us for a little while as they thought best; but God disciplines us for our good, that we may share in his holiness. No discipline seems pleasant at the time, but painful. Later on, however, it produces a harvest of righteousness and peace for those who have been trained by it.[2]*

The overarching principle is clear. God always disciplines us for our good. On a human level, parents discipline children in keeping with what they believe to be for the child's good. But parents are not perfect and sometimes make mistakes. God, on the other hand, is holy and perfect. His discipline is always for our ultimate good. His discipline is seldom pleasant and sometimes extremely painful, but His purpose is to guide us back to the pathway of righteousness and peace.

These two words, *righteousness* and *peace,* must never be separated. Peace, which means literally "to be at one with," is a heartfelt need. Most of us crave "inner peace"—a removal of all anxiety. We want our emotions, thoughts, desires, and actions to relate to each other harmoniously.

We also desire peace in our human relationships. So many people have said to me through the years, "I would give everything I own simply to have harmony with my spouse," or in some cases, "with my children." On a broader scale, many of the world's religions have as the central motif the idea of peace—being in harmony with the universe. However, as much as people might desire for all their relationships to be peaceable—from individual to international—such a dream remains elusive.

The reality is that there can be no peace on any level of human existence if we do not live in keeping with the Creator's design. Scripture calls us to live righteously by choosing the right path and obeying the rules of God because we believe they are designed for our well-being. When we walk in righteousness, we experience peace. This is always God's desire for us, and His discipline is for the purpose of moving us to this higher ideal. Such awareness does not remove the pain of discipline, but it does remind us that the discipline is an act of God's love.

WHEN GOD DISCIPLINES IN OUR LOVE LANGUAGE

Words of Affirmation

Brad has always thrived on words of affirmation. As a high school freshman he joined a rock band as the guitarist, and he felt accepted and approved by the band members. The band played at a few birthday parties, and Brad's parents gave him regular words of affirmation about his musical abilities. But when the band tried to put together a demo tape, they were never able to succeed and disbanded by the beginning of Brad's junior year.

Brad went on to other pursuits, but in college decided to major in music education. Although his parents continued to affirm him, he did not receive much encouragement from his teachers. His musical career floundered. Eventually he changed his major to business, and his grades greatly improved.

Brad had never given much thought to God or spiritual matters until after graduation when he secured a job with a small company owned and operated by passionate Christians. They started each morning with prayer. The company was permeated with the spirit of excitement and encouragement, and they complimented Brad's work. In addition, he heard more about God during the first six months of employment than he had heard his whole life, and he began to read the Bible for himself.

Reading through the book of John, Brad was drawn by Jesus' description of Himself as "the good shepherd [who] lays down his life for the sheep."[3] He also responded to Jesus' statement that, "I am the resurrection and the life. He who believes in me will live, even though he dies."[4] By the time Brad neared the end of John, one paragraph captured his full attention: "Jesus did many other miraculous signs in the presence of his disciples, which are not recorded in this book. But these are written that you may believe that Jesus is the Christ, the Son of God, and that by believing you may have life in his name."[5]

Brad said, "Something deep within me responded and I said aloud, 'I believe.' In that moment, my life was changed forever." Brad had made the God connection. The next six months were a tremendous adventure as Brad saturated himself with the teachings of Scripture. He decided to attend his employer's church, where he immediately enrolled in a class for new Christians. Soon he began to learn to share his life with God.

The part of the worship service Brad enjoyed most was the music. He was singing words he had never sung before, and they were expressing the true feelings of his heart. Because his primary love language was words of affirmation, it was only natural that he would want to join the choir. However, at the first rehearsal, he discovered he didn't have the gift of singing. When the music director realized that Brad was off-key and out of rhythm, he took time to try to help him, but to no avail. The director was kind but honest as he suggested Brad needed to find another area of ministry.

Brad's response was typical: "It was the most devastating experience I had encountered since becoming a Christian. At first I thought the music minister was out of line. Hadn't I been in a rock band in high school? Didn't I first major in music at college? But then a couple of friends confirmed his diagnosis, and I came to accept my musical limitations. I think the reason I felt so strongly was because I saw singing as a way of expressing praise to God. I was right, but I should have been singing in private rather than distracting fellow worshipers by singing off-key."

The good news is that Brad went on to become a successful businessman. He also found an outlet for his love language, words of affirmation, by becoming an energetic Bible teacher at his church. For the past twenty years, his classes have been well attended. People bring friends and they are never disappointed. Brad's classes are creative, alive, and insightful.

Words of affirmation remained his primary love language, and he expresses his love to God by teaching the truth of Scripture to hundreds of people every year. Yet it took the loving discipline of painful words from a music minister (and ultimately God) to steer Brad in a right and rewarding direction.

All people who have the primary love language of words of affirmation will find critical or corrective words very painful. But if they persistently seek to hear the voice of God, they may discover that such words are the clearest expressions of His love. Once God guides them to where they need to be, they will again hear affirming words from those to whom they minister.

Quality Time

Megan's primary love language is quality time. I first met her when she was a student majoring in religious studies. She had a deep passion for God and would spend hours in contemplation, meditation, and prayer. Conversations with her were always stimulating, and fellow students looked up to her as a spiritual guide. After graduation she spent two years working with a mission organization in South America. Later she returned and completed a master's degree in counseling.

About halfway through her program, she started dating a young man who prided himself in being agnostic. He was convinced that no one could be certain of God's existence. Six years had passed when Megan told me the story.

"I fell in love with him, and before I knew it, I too was doubting the existence of God. I stopped having my daily devotional times, and I started attending meetings where my boyfriend and others discussed an intellectual approach to life without a belief in God. At first

I thought I could be a positive influence on him and his friends, but as time went on I realized that they were having an influence on me. I noticed I was spending more time reading the books he recommended than I spent reading Scripture.

"I had a growing sense of emptiness and eventually realized that I was living only to be with my boyfriend and that our being together was the focus of my life. When he left me for another girl, I was devastated. By that time I had completed my master's degree in counseling, and I realized that I was in a deep, clinical depression. I tried to pray, but it seemed like God wasn't listening.

"I began treatment for my depression and started feeling better in about six months, but I still felt far away from God. In my heart I knew He was there, but the depression had left me with so many memories of loneliness that I wondered if I would ever experience God's presence again. About that time a friend invited me to a Bible study at her house. I went because I wanted to be around Christians again."

Megan said the next three months were "the most important of my life." After a long period of not experiencing God in her primary love language, she yearned for quality time with Him. Her sentiments echoed the writing of the psalmist: "As the deer pants for streams of water, so my soul pants for you, O God. My soul thirsts for God, for the living God. When can I go and meet with God?"[6]

Megan took home the workbook from the Bible study and prayed to start over as though she were just beginning her relationship with God. "It was like coming home from a long journey," she told me. "Day by day as I studied the Scriptures, I rediscovered the love of God. I realized the futility of life apart from Him. The highlight of my day was the time spent reading the Scriptures and talking to God. For two years I have continued to meet with my study group every week. I now have a job as a full-time counselor, and I've never been happier in my life."

It has been twenty years since that conversation with Megan. Today she is one of the finest counselors I know, and one of her specialties is helping people understand and process depression. She has married and given birth to two children, limiting her counseling to two days a week, but her passion for God has never wavered. Reflecting on her experience, she said, "The severe discipline of depression was the most significant event in my life. I shudder to think what would have happened to me if I had continued on the road I was walking. It was the desperation of depression that brought me back to God. As painful as it was, I sincerely thank Him for the experience."

God loves us enough to allow us to stray from Him for a while if that is what it takes to create a fresh hunger for His presence. People whose primary love language is quality time frequently sense His discipline in such situations.

Gifts

I remember a man who left his wife to pursue a relationship with another woman. After a few months he came to my office for help. He recounted how he had prayed and asked God to bless his new relationship, but instead his life had become miserable.

"At first it was exciting," he said. "But then I began to realize how many people I was hurting. One night I was praying out of deep pain and telling God how sorry I was. Then I asked His forgiveness. It was like God wrapped His arms around me and welcomed me home. Later, I realized that the anguish I had suffered was a gift from God. He loved me enough not to give me what I thought I wanted."

For those whose primary love language is gifts, answered prayer is strong, emotional evidence of God's love. In the early years of their spiritual journey, they may become troubled and even angry at God when they do not receive what they pray for. When their prayers seem to go unanswered, their faith in God is shaken. When they encounter tragedy, they think that God has been unfair. They tend to struggle more deeply with suffering and unanswered prayer than do other believers. But as they mature, they come to see even those things in a positive light.

They realize that just as loving parents do not always grant the requests of their children, God's refusal to give His children all that they request is not a withdrawal of His love. Sometimes what appears to be tragedy may actually be God's loudest expression of love.

Acts of Service

People whose primary love language is acts of service most often express their love to God by serving others in Jesus' name. If that opportunity is removed, they may experience a crisis of faith.

Robert's father was a reclusive manufacturer of electronic equipment who taught electronics at the local community college and spent his spare time in his basement shop. As a child, Robert seldom had his father's attention. His mother complained about her husband's lifestyle and spent much of her time depressed. She was extremely domineering and controlled Robert's life. During his teenage years, Robert began to realize that he was sexually attracted to young men, and by the time he was eighteen he was involved in a homosexual relationship.

Robert dreamed of the liberation college would provide. He could hardly wait to get away from his parents, enjoy his independence, and explore his sexuality. However, six weeks into the first semester Robert found himself very lonely and depressed. Little did he know that his life was about to take a radical turn.

Julia was a fellow freshman with a bubbly personality. She was an active Christian and had a natural inclination for helping people. Julia invited Robert to join her for her weekly Meals on Wheels commitment, and he was eager to help. Later she recruited him to help build a Habitat for Humanity house, and in the fall she pulled him into a leaf-raking, gutter-cleaning project sponsored by her Bible study group. Before the first semester was over, Robert was attending the group regularly, and in the second semester he made the God connection.

As he put it, "Julia worked me into the arms of Jesus. I loved helping people and I also loved the way Julia provided much-needed help with my math assignments. She seemed to genuinely care about me. Later she explained that she loved me because God first loved her, and that she enjoyed helping me because God had helped her, so I was interested in this God. I finally discovered what God had already done for me when He sent Christ to die for me. I realized that He loved me, and I knew that I must respond to His love."

Clearly, Robert's love language was acts of service, but in loving God, Robert didn't know what to do about his homosexual lifestyle. As he continued to study the Bible, he realized that homosexuality was not God's plan of sexual expression, but could not understand his strong attractions for other men. He eventually shared his struggles with Julia, even though he feared that she might reject him when she knew.

Her initial response shocked him. She gave him the longest, hardest hug he had ever received from anyone. Then she told him, "Oh, Robert. I'm so glad you are being honest with me. There is hope. God can take care of your problem." Robert wasn't as convinced, but he was willing to give God a chance. Julia introduced Robert to her pastor, who in turn referred him to a Christian counselor. The counselor helped Robert understand his sexual feelings and affirmed Julia's belief that distorted sexual feelings, like other distorted emotions, could be changed. For Robert, it was a life-changing experience that led not only to the diminishing of his attraction to the same sex, but also to the discovery and development of heterosexual feelings.

Robert continued to be active in the Bible study group with Julia and to participate in acts of service to the community. Upon graduation, he and Julia married and headed off to seminary. Robert believed that God wanted him to be a minister. After seminary he was eager to begin a full-time ministry using his primary love language in service for Christ, and was overjoyed when he was called to a small-town church in Virginia. However, three years later the church asked him to resign.

In his efforts to help others, Robert had been honest about his earlier struggles with homosexuality. When the deacons learned of his past, they did not want such a man to be their pastor. Robert's faith was greatly shaken—not only his faith in the Christians to whom he ministered, but his faith in God as well. He wondered whether God had forsaken him. He had come to the church so he could serve God; now his opportunity for service was gone. Where was God in all of this?

What Robert did not know was that God had far different plans for his life. Today he leads a thriving ministry to men and women who have suffered from same-sex attraction disorder. Many of them lived an active homosexual or lesbian lifestyle but have made the God connection and are coming to grips with the power of God to change lives. It is not a ministry that Robert would have chosen for himself. He would have preferred to leave that portion of his life behind him and use his energy to pastor a "normal" church. Yet he is discovering that the previous aspects of his life had uniquely prepared him for his current ministry. The humiliation of losing his first ministry enabled him to discover God's designed ministry for him.

Was the experience painful? Yes. Did the deacons violate Christian principles in their action? Yes. But God used those injustices to speak deeply to Robert's spirit and open his heart to a different ministry.

Sometimes sincere efforts to love God by serving others will be thwarted—perhaps by a direct act of Satan, perhaps by well-meaning

Christians. People with acts of service as a primary love language will react strongly to what they perceive as failures. But nothing can thwart the hand and voice of God, moving His children in the best direction for them. In some cases it may be the only discipline that fully captures their attention and motivates them to seek God's new directions for their lives.

Physical Touch

C. S. Lewis wrote in *The Problem of Pain*: "God whispers to us in our pleasures, speaks in our conscience, but shouts in our pain: it is his megaphone to rouse a deaf world."[7] Sickness is often God's email to turn our attention in a different direction. But for those whose primary love language is physical touch, it is God's megaphone. They are affected more deeply and their lives are more profoundly changed than others who have a different love language.

I met Clarence over forty years ago when he was at church in a wheelchair, afflicted with multiple sclerosis. Over the years his disease progressed in spite of numerous prayers for healing. Eventually he became bedridden, and during the last fifteen years of his life could no longer move his arms and legs. The only physical movement of his body that he could still control was in his neck.

The local library provided an apparatus that held a book above the bed, allowing him to read and turn the pages by placing his chin on a metal bar. A friend designed a similar mechanism whereby Clarence could turn on the radio using the same chin movement. But Clarence's contact with the outside world was essentially limited to a radio and books.

Periodically I visited Clarence and had many extended conversations, some of which focused on God's purposes in allowing him to suffer from multiple sclerosis. He had completed college and seminary in preparation for ministry and soon had a pastorate, but his preaching ministry was cut short. He had difficulty understanding that. As Paul had done, Clarence prayed for healing, but the healing he desired did not come. Instead he developed a growing awareness that God had a different kind of ministry for him, one that focused not on preaching, but on praying.

Clarence became one of the most devoted praying people I have ever known. As he listened to the radio, he prayed for the individual behind the voice and for the people who heard the message. Every page of every book brought to mind people for whom he needed to pray. As word spread that Clarence was a prayer warrior, requests came from many quarters. I often shared my own needs and always knew in my heart that, for him, prayer requests were never a burden, but a ministry.

For twenty-five years, Clarence had an unparalleled ministry of prayer, the results of which only eternity will reveal. First seated in his chair and later prone on his bed, he continued to search for understanding concerning God's purpose for his life. Even though he lost the joy of physical touch, Clarence's suffering became a megaphone through which God spoke to channel his life into the most productive ministry possible for him.

ASKING "WHY?"

Sometimes God's discipline seems harshest when our hopes or expectations go unfulfilled. During those times it is especially important to remember that God is good and He still loves us. I remember Cindy, whom I met at a large single adult conference. She said, "I used to think God didn't love me because He hadn't given me a husband. For years I prayed diligently for 'the right man,' but God never answered my prayer. My friends were getting married, and I often felt that God must love them more than me. But then, one by one, I saw my friends get divorced after seven, ten, twelve years of marriage. I saw the pain they endured and the trauma created in the lives of their children. Their pain was far worse than the pain I had felt in my singleness. I remember the day I said to God, 'It's okay, Father. In fact, thank You for not answering my prayer in giving me a husband. I realize now that I would have been too immature to have succeeded in marriage. Thank You for the gift of singleness.'"

At that conference, Cindy was genuinely happy to be single. She didn't feel that God had slighted her, but had loved her intently and preserved her from tragedy. Yet within a year of that conversation, I got a letter from Cindy: "Dear Dr. Chapman, I am writing to say that God has finally brought the right man into my life. I really wasn't anticipating marriage. I'm sure you remember our conversation, but it just happened. I met Kevin shortly after I left the conference last year. He had only arrived in our city about a month earlier and immediately joined our singles' group at church. We became friends three months before we dated. And our relationship has been everything I ever dreamed of. Kevin is truly a Christian gentleman. Isn't God good?"

Cindy and Kevin have been married for ten years now and have two children and a delightful relationship. They periodically lead marriage enrichment groups in their church. Cindy once said to me, "God gives good gifts to His children, but only when He knows they are ready to receive them."

A persistent question arises when those who seek to follow God are confronted with physical pain and/or debilitating disease: *If God is love, then why does He allow His children to suffer such intense pain?*

In grappling with this difficult question, sincere Christians have come to different conclusions. Some propose that all sickness and suffering is from Satan, that it is never God's will for His people to experience disease. Therefore, if Satan inflicts sickness, then the prayer of faith should bring healing. Although there are legitimate testimonies of divine healing, there are also thousands of people whose relationship with God was shaken or shattered after they "prayed in faith" and were not healed.

It is true that the Scriptures instruct believers to pray for the healing of the sick, yet God has not categorically committed Himself to heal every person who expresses faith. A person's willingness to believe may be one factor, but healing rests solidly in the hands of the sovereign God who chooses to heal or not to heal, always acting for our good and the good of others.

Paul was the first-century apostle who became the greatest leader of the early Christian church. It could be argued that he was perhaps the most faithful and committed person of his time, yet he was not spared suffering and pain. He was often thrown into prison and flogged severely. One time he was stoned and left for dead. Three times he was shipwrecked. He underwent regular danger from his spiritual opponents, from robbers, and from other sources. Though clearly unpleasant, none of those challenges seemed to trouble Paul deeply.

However, Paul did struggle when his body was afflicted with disease. Three times he pleaded with God for healing, but rather than heal him, God's response was, "My grace is sufficient for you, for my power is made perfect in weakness." Upon reflection, Paul concluded that his illness was to keep him from becoming conceited because of the great revelations God had given him. He saw his physical malady as God's positive, loving discipline. As a result, he was able to say, "Therefore I will boast all the more gladly about my weaknesses, so that Christ's power may rest on me. That is why, for Christ's sake, I delight in weaknesses, in insults, in hardships, in persecutions, in difficulties. For when I am weak, then I am strong."[8]

Throughout history many Christian leaders, like Paul, have experienced the pain of disease and/or suffering. Typically, such experiences draw attention to God, particularly after medical professionals have done all they can do and the disease persists.

I suspect that Paul's primary love language was probably physical touch. His conversion had been precipitated by the presence of God touching his body, leaving him blind for three days. After his conversion, he was a man on the move, physically pouring out his life as an expression of love for Christ, the One who had touched him and turned his life around. In the midst of Paul's fruitful ministry, God used the loving discipline of physical touch to keep him on track so that the latter portion of his life would be fully as effective as the early years following his conversion.

At the end of his life Paul could say, "The time has come for my departure. I have fought the good fight, I have finished the race, I have kept the faith."[9] God's loving discipline had served its purpose, and Paul had nothing but gratitude in response.

I want to reiterate: God's discipline is not always in response to sinful behavior. Often it is His method of redirecting our sincere efforts to worship and serve Him. Though our initial response may be to recoil in pain and question what He is doing, if we continue to listen for His voice, we will likely discover that it is during our moments of deepest pain when we experience God's love most intensely. And when we eventually comprehend His plan, we find more peace and satisfaction with life than we had ever known.

QUESTIONS FOR REFLECTION / DISCUSSION

(1) When you hear the word *discipline*, what first comes to your mind?

(2) Think of various ways your parents disciplined you as a child. As you think back on them as an adult, did most of those attempts have a positive or a negative effect on you?

(3) Can you think of a time when God used your primary love language to discipline you in some way? What were the circumstances? What was the result?

Chapter Ten

WHATEVER *the* LANGUAGE, *Let* LOVE PREVAIL

I first encountered Michael Cassidy in the breathtakingly beautiful Sheldonian Theater at Oxford University in England. He was introduced as one of the top twenty people in South Africa who eased the transition from apartheid to free elections. I was captivated by his story.

He said, "I came to Cambridge to study law, but within two weeks I encountered Christ." Shortly thereafter, Billy Graham visited Cambridge and Michael was encouraged and inspired in his newfound Christian faith. Cassidy completed his Cambridge studies, came to the United States for theological studies, and then felt called to return to South Africa. His vision was to conduct citywide evangelistic crusades similar to those of Dr. Graham.

He had grown up in South Africa, a nation with a largely nonwhite population whose government was dominated by whites, part of the entrenched system of apartheid.

"Apartheid, I was convinced, was evil," Cassidy said. "I knew I had to face the fire of opposing it." Earlier in his graduate studies in seminary, he had become convinced that the gospel of Christ had a balanced commitment to the saving of souls and the dignity of human life. Spiritual concern could not be separated from social concern. "Justice is love built into structures," Cassidy said. He reminded the audience that John and Charles Wesley had challenged unjust structures and eventually the slavery trade was abolished. "Moral change brought social change," he said.

Twenty million people in South Africa called themselves Christians, but most had little interest in applying Christianity to social structures of life. God's word to the prophet Jeremiah became Cassidy's guiding light: "'For I know the plans I have for you,' declares the Lord, 'plans to prosper you and not to harm you, plans to give you hope and a future. Then you will call upon me and come and pray to me, and I will listen to you. You will seek me and find me when you seek me with all your heart.'"[1]

Cassidy said, "These words were spoken to Israel in the darkest hour of Babylonian captivity. God had plans for ancient Israel, and we knew God had plans for us. We are a people of hope, and we knew that God was already at work in South Africa." Yet when he decided to tackle apartheid head-on, the years that followed were difficult. As a leader in the antiapartheid movement, he was accused by police of working for the CIA. And his nephew was sentenced to six years in prison after refusing to fight in the apartheid army.

Cassidy's opposition came not only from government leaders but also from many white Christians who were satisfied with the status quo. But he remained convinced that people should have a sense of moral order because they are created in God's image, and God exemplifies complete righteousness. Only God could touch the hearts of people and bring all parties to a peaceful resolution. Even though Cassidy believed that "apartheid was against the grain of the universe," his great challenge was "to come in love."

So in April 1983 Cassidy called the nation to prayer. He headed a prayer chain that focused on praying for the nation. For two years, day and night around the clock, Christians prayed for God's direction in their nation. All across the nation, people prayed—including forty-two inmates on death row.

Cassidy and those who worked with him also began to organize weekend retreats, bringing together equal numbers of whites and non-whites. These were retreats of politicians from the far right and the far left and everyone in between. The meetings focused on sharing their personal stories. One black Christian, who had been a political prisoner on the notorious Robben Island, where Nelson Mandela spent most of his prison years, shared his experience of being buried up to his neck in a pit with only his head above the soil, and then having white men urinate on him. As such atrocities were revealed, the hearts of whites and nonwhites began to soften and the walls of hostility started to disintegrate. Church leaders began to get involved in the call for justice.

In 1985 Christians were challenged to stay home from work and invest the day in prayer. That day of prayer brought the nation to a standstill, but it turned the country's focus to God. When in due time the political leaders eventually agreed to seek to work out a new agreement for the nation's political process, there was much tension. Despite much negotiation, it seemed that the whole process would fall apart. At that point, Cassidy and others organized a prayer meeting at a rugby stadium. Over thirty thousand came to pray. While the political leaders met in the VIP lounge of the stadium, Christians out on the field prayed for a breakthrough, not knowing of the meeting in the lounge. Later the media would report that "the Jesus peace rally" turned the tide. The nation was allowed free elections that took place in peace.

In Cassidy's words, "We had to face the reality that only God could change the hearts of men and remove apartheid in a peaceful way. It required confessions and repentance, but God intervened in human history. Great things happen on the wheels of relationships."[2]

When love prevails, human social structures can change. We can move closer to the ideal of justice, realizing that what Cassidy said is true: "Justice is love built into structures." Only love has the potential of bringing human societies to a higher level of justice, according to Cassidy. However, because of the reality of evil, such love will never be expressed without opposition.

Not all of the problems of South Africa have abated since the establishment of free elections. Love has not always prevailed, but where there are people who genuinely love God, human relationships will continue to improve. Cassidy was right. "Great things happen on the wheels of relationships." And the oil that lubricates the wheels of relationships is love. No power holds more potential for changing human relationships than the power of love.

"I PRAYED FOR GOD TO PUT US WHERE HE WANTED US"

On an individual level, a person's love for God may dramatically alter his or her plans. Dr. Larry Pepper (in this case, Dr. Pepper is the actual name) worked as a flight surgeon for the National Aeronautics and Space Administration (NASA) and was involved in the medical selection of astronauts at the Johnson Space Center in Houston. He shuttled to Florida's Kennedy Space Center for launches, heading up emergency medical teams in case of accidents and assisting in crew recovery after landings. He worked more than fifteen missions, including the first Hubble Space Telescope repair mission, and he dreamed of someday making a space flight.

In 1996, however, Larry committed to a totally different vocational track. He had been active in his local church, deeply committed to Jesus Christ, in the midst of a successful career, and helping his wife, Sally, raise their three children. But at that point he received a message from God. In Larry's own words, the message was, "'You've committed everything to Me—except your job.'

"That was the turning point," he says. "I prayed and told God that I wanted Him to put us where He wanted us to be."

Larry and Sally began to pray for God's direction. In a few months, Larry went on a volunteer trip to Zaire to work with Rwandan refugees. There he met Larry Pumpelly, a missionary who told him about the need for doctors at Mbarara University Hospital—a teaching facility in Uganda. Larry knew in his heart this was God's direction. Yet, after making the decision to become a missionary, he was selected as a finalist for astronaut duty in space. He saw this news as a test of whether he really loved God more than his former dream.

Love prevailed and since 1996, Larry and Sally have been demonstrating the love of God to patients and interns alike, half a world away in Uganda. Among other achievements to date, he has instituted an AIDS outpatient clinic.

"We're offering something other AIDS organizations don't do by dealing with the spiritual aspect," Larry said. He expressed great comfort in knowing that although most of his AIDS patients would die, many would first discover the assurance of God's love and the anticipation of eternal life. As he trains young national physicians, he seeks to demonstrate what it means to be a Christian physician committed to dispensing the love of God along with medical help. He leads a weekly Bible study for interns, focusing on the needs of Ugandan men. On Friday evenings, he and Sally offer an alternative to the Mbarara bar scene, providing medical students with an opportunity to play games, watch movies, and discuss biblical concepts.

On Sunday mornings, the Peppers lead their "church." Sally prepares the prenatal clinic at the hospital for church services and leads children in a Bible study. After Larry checks on his patients, he leads a worship service. On Sunday evenings, Larry and Sally lead a coed Bible study where they seek to make practical the teachings of Jesus to young Ugandan medical personnel.[3] They are a couple who demonstrate every day how love has prevailed in their lives.

LOOKING BEYOND THE RUBBISH

After hearing a number of stories about Africa, I was able to make my own journey awhile back. I went to the West African country of Benin and stayed in a small hotel in the coastal city of Cotonou. At first there was no water. The official word from downstairs was, "We have ordered the part. It will be in tomorrow."

I was feeling somewhat frustrated until I turned my thoughts to God. I was reminded almost immediately that if I was feeling helpless and that my life was out of control, perhaps I should reflect upon the hundreds of thousands of black men and women who sailed from these very shores against their will to work on the plantations owned by my ancestors. I wrote the following passage in my journal:

"As I sit here in West Africa and realize the atrocity of slavery and how the Christian church in England and America bought into that unholy practice, my heart is saddened. I wonder that the blacks of our generation could ever hear the love of God through white vessels. Only God Himself can help any of us look beyond the rubbish and see the Redeemer."

In every generation, there are those who claim to be "lovers of God" whose behavior belies their profession. They are those who pollute the river of God's love. But every generation also has its John Wesleys, William Wilberforces, Harriet Beecher Stowes, and thousands of others whose names never make the history books. They are voices calling out of the darkness to say human exploitation is wrong, whatever the motive. Christ came to save, never to exploit. He made a distinction between mere profession of faith and true possession of faith. Talking the talk is not the same as walking the walk. As one of Jesus' own disciples wrote: "How can you say that you love God whom you have not seen when you do not love your brother whom you have seen?"[4]

Sitting in that third-floor hotel room, I was reminded of the atrocities of the past. But then I also thought of the thousands of true followers of Jesus who had come to these same shores simply to share His love. If one were to traverse this huge continent, he would encounter literally thousands of hospitals, clinics, colleges and universities, medical schools, and social service projects started by missionaries who loved God more than an easy life.

West Africa is not called "the graveyard of missionaries" without cause. Among the small group of missionaries with whom I met, one had lost his wife when she was thirty-two. Almost all had experienced malaria at least once. Four had been held at gunpoint, gagged, and robbed. Many lived in extremely remote villages that were inaccessible during the rainy season. But all had a passion for God and a love that could not be stopped.

Those people were not explorers whose thrill came from discovering a new waterfall; they were men and women who have experienced the love of God through Jesus Christ. They were investing their lives in taking that love to others. And wherever they go, love always prevails.

GOD'S LOVE: EVERLASTING AND UNCONDITIONAL

Love involves seeking the well-being of another. Because people are made in the image of God and God's nature is characterized by love, something in the heart of every person knows that love is the right thing to do.

However, people are also estranged from God, and in our natural state we tend to love those who love us. "I will seek your well-being as long as you seek my well-being" is the rule of the day for individuals as well as many of the world's religions.

Jesus was radical in His teaching. He told one such religious group, "You have heard that it was said, 'Love your neighbor and hate your enemy.' But I tell you: Love your enemies and pray for those who persecute you." The basis of His noble challenge was God Himself. Jesus said, "[God] causes his sun to rise on the evil and the good, and sends rain on the righteous and the unrighteous. If you love those who love you, what reward will you get? . . . And if you greet only your brothers, what are you doing more than others? Do not even pagans do that?"[5]

Jesus made clear distinctions between religiously motivated love and divinely motivated love. Those who have made the God connection will never be satisfied with merely loving those who love them in return.

The question is how to break free from the gravity of earthly love to experience the freedom of divine love. I am convinced that the answer lies in bringing our weakness to the One who has strength, namely, Jesus of Nazareth.

To a group of religious people who claimed to have a relationship with God, Jesus said:

"If God were your father, you would love me, for I came from God and now am here. I have not come on my own; but he sent me. Why is my language not clear to you? Because you are unable to hear what I say. You belong to your father, the devil, and you want to carry out your father's desire. He

was a murderer from the beginning, not holding to the truth, for there is no truth in him. When he lies, he speaks his native language, for he is a liar and the father of lies. Yet because I tell you the truth, you do not believe me! Can any of you prove me guilty of sin? If I am telling the truth, why don't you believe me? He who belongs to God hears what God says. The reason you do not hear is that you do not belong to God."[6]

His would have been extremely harsh words if they weren't true. However, because they *were* true, they explain why religious people have often been involved in murder and lying. They are simply following the example of their father, the devil. They are sincere people, but are sincerely wrong.

The answer to humankind's dilemma is not to unify the world's religions and bring them together into one great world religion that will institute peace. The world's religions, whether individually or corporately, have never led people to experience the kind of divine love of which Jesus spoke. No religion, even the "Christian" religion, has ever produced such love. This kind of love flows only through those who have made the genuine God connection, those who truly follow Christ. Like Christ, they have learned to "look to . . . the interests of others" and "honor one another above [them]selves."[7]

The apostle Paul, who himself was caught up in religion before his genuine God connection, put it this way: "Very rarely will anyone die for a righteous man, though for a good man someone might possibly dare to die. But God demonstrates his own love for us in this: While we were still sinners, Christ died for us."[8]

Human love might motivate us to sacrifice, or even die, for someone whom we consider good. For example, one sibling might donate an organ to another, or parents might be willing to die in order to save the life of a child. But human love does not lift us to the level of dying for our enemies. This degree of love flows only from God, who makes it available to us. Again Paul wrote, "God has poured out his love into our hearts by the Holy Spirit, whom he has given us."[9]

The Scriptures are clear. God loves us with an everlasting love. He loves us even though we have turned away from Him and walked our own way. Yet our human willful rebellion creates problems. Because God is totally righteous and holy, He cannot accept our sinfulness. To do so would violate His justice. So human sin results in a chasm between people and God.

It is not unlike what happens when one spouse is unfaithful to the other. A gulf forms between the two individuals and the sense of distance is inevitable. Even our limited human sense of justice demands payment for wrongdoing, so we should certainly expect no less from God's perfect justice. However, God's love is perfect as well, so His love for humankind motivated Him to send Jesus, who endured the full penalty for our wrongdoing. Thus, the demands of justice were met at the cross of Jesus Christ.

From a human point of view, Jesus died at the age of thirty-three at the hands of religious people. However, from heaven's perspective, His death was an act of love to pay for the sins of all who would accept God's forgiveness. He had not come to earth to live a long life as a celebrated teacher. He had come to die, which is why He could say from the cross moments before He died, "It is finished."[10] What happened at that moment and three days later has forever changed the lives of those who believe. The historical record is clear.

The curtain of the temple was torn in two from top to bottom. The earth shook and the rocks split. The tombs broke open and the bodies of many holy people who had died were raised to life. They came out of the tombs, and after Jesus' resurrection they went into the holy city and appeared to many people. When the centurion and those with him who were guarding Jesus saw the earthquake and all that happened, they were terrified, and exclaimed, "Surely he was the Son of God!"[11]

The curtain in the temple prevented access to the Most Holy Place (sometimes called the Holy of Holies) where the Ark of the Covenant was kept. Only the high priest was permitted into the Most Holy Place, and then only once a year to offer an animal sacrifice for the sins of the people. The annual ritual was symbolic of Jesus, the Lamb of God, whom the Scriptures say was "slain from the creation of the world."[12]

Jesus has existed in eternity past with God the Father, yet when He invaded human history in the form of a man to offer Himself as a sacrifice, temple sacrifices were no longer needed. The symbolic action had given way to the reality of God's forgiveness for all people who believed.

The resurrection of Jesus from the dead is documented as well as any event in ancient history. Again and again, those who have examined the evidence have arrived at the same conclusion: Jesus was raised from the dead three days after He died on a cross. His resurrection is the supernatural evidence that His words were to be trusted. Those who believe and respond receive God's forgiveness and the gift of the Holy Spirit. God's Spirit comes to reside in them, and they experience the love of God to share with their generation. This is what Paul meant when he wrote in Romans 5:5, "God has poured out his love into our hearts by the Holy Spirit, whom he has given us." In addition, those who believe can also look forward to resurrection after death and eternity with God in heaven.

If you are encountering these ideas for the first time, I know they seem to be incredible. But I know also that because you are made in God's image and because God loves you, there is something within your spirit that affirms, "Yes, this is truth." Acting on this response allows you to make the God connection. The words you say to God are unimportant, but the heart cry of many believers is something like this: "Lord, I find it difficult to believe that You love me so much, but I open my heart to You. I want to accept Your forgiveness. I thank You that Christ has paid my penalty. I invite Your Spirit into my life. I want my life to be a channel of Your love. I give myself to You forever."

Thousands of people from cultures around the globe have made that kind of response to God and by so doing have found love and life forever. Through the lives of those individuals, the love of God is spoken in all five love languages around the world in every generation. One by one, people continue to respond to the love of God and make "the God connection."

MY UNLIKELY FRIENDSHIP

For almost forty years now, one of my closest friends has been Clarence Shuler. We were both born in the Deep South before the days of integration, Clarence to black parents and I to white, so the likelihood of our forming a friendship in the late 1960s was not very great. Racial tensions were high; integration of public schools was not being accepted without resistance. The cultural climate did not foster interracial relationships.

I was serving on the staff of an all-white church that had just completed a new gymnasium. During one "fun night for teens," Clarence and his friend Russell walked into the gymnasium. I could not help but notice them, so I went over, introduced myself, and welcomed them to the evening. They seemed to have a good time and began to attend meetings regularly.

Clarence participated freely in discussions and was not afraid to ask questions. He always had a cordial spirit. When it came time for the youth retreat, Clarence signed up. During that weekend, Clarence would make the God connection. Friday night and Saturday were filled with fun activities. On Saturday night, I gave a lecture and ended with the question, "Is your life complete or is something missing?" Clarence later said, "I had already realized that something was missing in my life. I had thought that if I could make the high school basketball team, all my problems would be solved. Well, after I made the team, I quickly realized that I still had the same problems! I needed Jesus Christ in my life."

I shall never forget the night that Clarence and I bowed on the ground behind a pickup truck as he asked Jesus Christ to forgive him of his sins and to come into his life. Clarence says of that experience, "My life really changed! God gave me an inner peace that has stayed with me no matter what the situation. God taught me the freedom of being an individual so that I no longer had to follow the crowd to find acceptance. Most of all, I began to live the wonderful life God had planned for me." However, he would eventually confess, "As excited as I was to have become a Christian, it bothered me that a white man led me to Christ. Later, I realized that to him race didn't matter, and that it shouldn't matter to me. All that mattered was that Christ was now in my life!"

Clarence continued to be active in our youth group and began to study the Scriptures for himself. At that time, Karolyn and I had "open house" for college students every Friday night, which he started attending regularly. He began to memorize Scripture and share his faith with others. When summer rolled around, I asked if he would be willing to serve as a counselor at our church camp. We assigned him a group of thirteen-year-old boys, all white. Clarence said, "That's an experience I'll never forget."

Clarence graduated from high school and then completed college and seminary. Since then he has worked with a variety of Christian organizations as a cross-cultural consultant. He has authored five books and numerous articles. He is a devoted husband and father.

Clarence has often publicly and privately expressed appreciation for my role in his life. He extols me for my bravery in the late '60s by making him feel welcomed in an all-white church, but I think he was the brave one. He taught me much of divine love. He has shown me that love covers a multitude of sins, that love transcends racial boundaries, and that love is always willing to forgive. God showed love to me by bringing Clarence Shuler into my life.

I have come to believe that the only solution to the racial tensions of my country and others around the world is divine love. I understand full well that people cannot give what they have not received. The answer is not more sermons on love; the answer is helping people one at a time make the God connection. Once an individual knows God and is controlled by His Spirit, love will flow freely through him or her.

BECOMING "MULTILINGUAL"

Jesus taught those who followed Him while He was on earth, "A new command I give you: Love one another. As I have loved you, so you must love one another. By this all men will know that you are my disciples, if you love one another."[13] Love is the distinguishing mark of those who follow Jesus. If we are to be God's agents to help others come to know Him in a personal way, it will not be through arguments or force, but through divine love.

Years ago Nicky Cruz was a drug-addicted gang leader on the streets of New York City. He was approached by David Wilkerson, a young, passionate follower of Jesus.

"You come near me, Preacher, and I'll kill you," Nicky warned.

"You could do that. You could cut me in a thousand pieces and lay them out in the street and every piece would love you," Wilkerson responded.[14]

In time, Nicky became a follower of Jesus. Love prevails.

We come to God as individuals, but once the God connection is made, He places us into His family. For the rest of our lives and throughout eternity, we are never again alone. We belong to each other, and together we reach out to those not yet in the family and become God's agents of love to them.[15]

Whatever love language God speaks to draw us to Him will be the love language we most naturally use to express our love to God. But we must not stop there. As we continue an incredible love relationship with God, it is His desire that we learn to receive His love in all five languages. The apostle Paul expressed it this way:

> For this reason I kneel before the Father, from whom his whole family in heaven and on earth derives its name. I pray that out of his glorious riches he may strengthen you with power through his Spirit in your inner being, so that Christ may dwell in your hearts through faith. And I pray that you, being rooted and established in love, may have power, together with all the saints, to grasp how wide and long and high and deep is the love of Christ, and to know this love that surpasses knowledge—that you may be filled to the measure of all the fullness of God.
>
> Now to him who is able to do immeasurably more than all we ask or imagine, according to his power that is at work within us, to him be glory in the church and in Christ Jesus throughout all generations, for ever and ever! Amen.[16]

Scripture is clear that making the God connection is not a culmination, but rather a beginning. It also becomes clear that this love relationship with God involves an ongoing association with other members of the family. So as we learn to receive the love of God in all five love languages, we also begin to speak those languages to other believers as well as those not yet in God's family.

Expressing love using your primary love language will come naturally for you. Learning to speak the other four love languages may require more time and effort. However, we must remember that we don't generate the love, but simply channel the love that God provides.

We do not love others in order to be accepted by God; we love them in response to God's first loving us and graciously accepting us into His family. Learning to communicate love in all five love languages enhances our usefulness in the community of God. When love prevails in the Christian community, the non-Christian world will beat a path to our doors, for they desperately long for such love. Again, hear the words of Jesus: "A new command I give you: Love one another. As I have loved you, so you must love one another. By this all men will know that you are my disciples, if you love one another."[17]

Love is the distinguishing mark of the Christian. When God's love flows through us in all five love languages, we become surprisingly effective instruments in helping others make the God connection and enter His family. Despite any other challenges or obstacles we may face, love prevails!

QUESTIONS FOR REFLECTION / DISCUSSION

(1) Recall a time or two in your past when you would say that love prevailed in an unusual or difficult situation. What did you learn from each experience?

(2) Can you think of a time when you reached out in love across cultural, racial, or other barriers? Sometimes we see the results of such actions, as in the story about Clarence. Other times we don't see any immediate benefits from our faithfulness to God. What were the results of your efforts?

(3) Occasionally we get set in our ways and/or stop seeing opportunities to reach out to others with love. Think of the past week. Can you recall any chances you had to speak a love language to show God's love to others, but didn't? If so, what kept you from doing so? (Shyness? Fear? Too busy? Etc.) If you have a similar opportunity this week, what might you do differently to let love prevail?

The GOD

WHO SPEAKS *Your*

LANGUAGE

On September 11, 2001, terrorists hijacked four jetliners. Almost four thousand American citizens died in New York and Washington, D.C., at the hands of deluded religious zealots. Even now that several years have passed, the event stands as a tragic reminder that human religions do not hold the key to peace.

The purpose of this book is not to call people to greater religious devotion. Too often, the human exercise of religion has little to do with love. The religions of the world reveal our search for the transcendent, but they do not quench the thirst of the human soul. Christianity, when practiced as merely a religion, is no different. Thousands who call themselves Christians have never made the "God connection." I consider such people "cultural Christians." For them, Christianity is a set of beliefs and religious practices, such as attending church, giving money, repeating prayers, and trying to be good citizens. They hope that when they die they will go to heaven, but they have no assurance because they have no relationship with the God of heaven. They consider themselves Christian because they grew up in a home where their parents' religion was Christianity.

In this respect, they are no different from cultural Buddhists, Hindus, Jews, or Muslims. The religion of their parents is the religion of convenience. They acknowledge their longings for the transcendent, and their religion provides a vehicle for expressing spiritual hunger—yet the hunger is never truly satiated.

Religion often inoculates the individual from making the true "God connection." Some people say, "I have my own religion" while refusing to even consider a personal response to the love of God. In such cases, religion is just another tool of Satan that prevents people from experiencing true spiritual freedom.

However, people who are willing to look beyond their cultural religion and search for the genuine love of God will be rewarded. God's promise to those people is, "You will seek me and find me when you seek for me with all your heart. I will be found by you."[1]

GOD REVEALS LOVE

The God who revealed His love to the patriarchs and prophets is the same God who expressed His love supremely by wrapping Himself in human flesh beneath a Bethlehem star. He is the same God who demonstrated His love to humble fishermen (Peter, James, and John), tax collectors (Matthew), physicians (Luke), and religious zealots (Paul). He is the same God who is at work in the world today and continues to express His love to people like those I have described in this book. The good news is He loves you and me as much as anyone else. We are made in His image, and He longs to have a relationship with us.

And what I hope you realize by now is that He expresses His love to you in your own primary love language:

- To those who prefer the love language of words of affirmation, Jesus says, *"Come to me, all you who are weary and burdened, and I will give you rest. Take my yoke upon you and learn from me, for I am gentle and humble in heart, and you will find rest for your souls. For my yoke is easy and my burden is light."*[2]

- To those whose primary love language is gifts, Jesus says, *"My sheep listen to my voice; I know them, and they follow me. I give them eternal life, and they shall never perish; no one can snatch them out of my hand."*[3]

- To those who desire quality time, the Scriptures say, *"Come near to God and he will come near to you."*[4]

- To those whose love language is acts of service, Jesus says of Himself, *"The Son of Man did not come to be served, but to serve, and to give his life as a ransom for many." When those who knew Him best tried to summarize His life, they simply said, "He went around doing good and healing all who were under the power of the devil, because God was with him."*[5]

- For those who understand best the love language of physical touch, nothing speaks more profoundly than the incarnation of Christ. Here is the way John the apostle described it: *"[What] we have heard . . . seen with our eyes . . . looked at and our hands have touched—this we proclaim."* John also described Jesus' physical presence: *"We have seen his glory, the glory of the One and Only, who came from the Father, full of grace and truth."*[6]

God became human in order to touch us. As we read about the brief thirty-three years of His earthly journey, we find Him touching children, those afflicted with leprosy, the blind, and the deaf. His touch brought healing and hope to all whom He encountered.

We who live in the twenty-first century do not have the benefit of observing the life and teachings of Jesus, but we do have the record of what He said and did. Jesus clearly claimed that His teachings came from God: "If anyone loves me, he will obey my teaching. My Father will love him, and we will come to him and make our home with him. He who does not love me will not obey my teaching. These words you hear are not my own; they belong to the Father who sent me."[7] Jesus also indicated that once He had gone back to God His Father, He would send the Holy Spirit, who would "remind you of everything I have said to you."[8]

The New Testament was written by faithful people whose words were guided by the Spirit of God. Many were eyewitnesses who had seen the example Jesus had set and heard His teachings firsthand. John walked with Jesus for three and one-half years, and wrote that it would be impossible to record everything that Jesus said and did. But he stated clearly, "These are written that you may believe that Jesus is the Christ, the Son of God and that by believing you may have life in his name."[9]

GOD INITIATES LOVE

John also informs us that it was God who initiated love. "We love because he first loved us. If anyone says, 'I love God,' yet hates his brother, he is a liar. For anyone who does not love his brother, whom he has seen, cannot love God, whom he has not seen. And he has given us this command: Whoever loves God must also love his brother."[10]

In this passage, John was echoing the words of Jesus who had been asked by the religious leaders of His day to point out the greatest commandment in the Law. He answered, "'Love the Lord your God with all your heart and with all your soul and with all your mind.' This is the first and greatest commandment. And the second is like it: 'Love your neighbor as yourself.' All the Law and the Prophets hang on these two commandments."[11]

John also wrote:

Dear friends, let us love one another, for love comes from God. Everyone who loves has been born of God and knows God. Whoever does not love does not know God, because God is love. This is how God showed his love among us: He sent his one and only Son into the world that we might live through him. This is love: not that we loved God, but that he loved us and sent his Son as an atoning sacrifice for our sins.[12]

Paul did not see Christ in the flesh, but was "touched" by Him while he was en route to persecute believers. The love of Christ dramatically changed his life and priorities. He wrote:

The God who made the world and everything in it is the Lord of heaven and earth and does not live in temples built by hands. And he is not served by human hands, as if he needed anything, because he himself gives all men life and breath and everything else. From one man he made every nation of men, that they should inhabit the whole earth; and he determined the times set for them and the exact places where they should live. God did this so that men would seek him and perhaps reach out for him and find him, though he is not far from each one of us. "For in him we live and move and have our being. . . . We are his offspring."

Therefore since we are God's offspring, we should not think that the divine being is like gold or silver or stone—an image made by man's design and skill. In the past God overlooked such ignorance, but now he commands all people everywhere to repent. For he has set a day when he will judge the world with justice by the man he has appointed. He has given proof of this to all men by raising [Jesus] from the dead.[13]

GOD *IS* LOVE

As an author, I am aware that all I have written in this book about the love of God is but a note in the symphony of God's immeasurable love. The songwriter expressed it well:

Could we with ink the ocean fill,
And were the skies of parchment made,
Were every stalk on earth a quill,
And every man a scribe by trade;
To write the love of God above
Would drain the ocean dry;
Nor could the scroll contain the whole,
Tho' stretched from sky to sky.[14]

God has spoken and continues to speak His love in all languages. His message is clear: "I love you even though you have walked away from Me. I desire to forgive you. That is why I have paid for your wrongdoing. I want to have a love relationship with you. If you are willing to turn from your self-seeking path and accept My forgiveness and love, you will be My child forever. I will love you and give you the best possible life both now and for eternity. Open your heart to My love and My Spirit, and I will come to live with you." This is God's desire expressed throughout the Scriptures.

The message of God's grace (unmerited favor) and unconditional love seems incredible. By nature, people want to do something to earn God's forgiveness and to make peace with God. Yet all we can do is respond to what He has already done.

In every generation and in every culture, the Spirit of God continues to communicate divine love by speaking the love languages of God. God is both holy and loving. He reaches out in perfect love to offer forgiveness and the gift of an eternal relationship with Him. Those who reject His love must face His judgment. The fork in the road for all humankind is to choose God's love or God's justice. We either attempt to pay for our own wrongdoing—a debt we can never pay—or we accept the loving provision of God's payment on our behalf. The Son of God Himself made that payment. God's love and justice met on the cross of Jesus Christ, bringing life and forgiveness to all who believe.

The cross has become the universal symbol of God's love. The crucifixion of Jesus was a time when God clearly spoke all five love languages:

• From the cross Jesus said, "Father, forgive them, for they do not know what they are doing." What *affirming words* could speak more deeply of love? [15]

• In His death, Jesus performed His greatest *act of service* as He reconciled sinful humanity to the holy God. [16]

• He offered *gifts* of inestimable value: forgiveness of sins and eternal life. [17]

• His gifts provided the opportunity for people to have an intimate relationship with God by spending *quality time* with the Creator, both now and forever.

• And it was on the cross where God *touched* humanity at our point of deepest need and said, "I love you!" Here Jesus fulfilled His promise: "I am the good shepherd. The good shepherd lays down his life for the sheep." [18]

Our part is to simply lift our hands and receive His love. John described the nature of God simply and succinctly: "God is love." And he soon added: "We love because He first loved us." [19]

As we respond to the love of God and begin to identify the variety of languages He uses to speak to us, we soon learn to speak those languages ourselves. Whatever love language you prefer, may you find ever deeper satisfaction in using that language in your relationship with God and with other people.

NOTES

Introduction
The Love Connection

1. *World Book Encyclopedia,* 1970, s.v. "God."
2. Genesis 1:27.

Chapter 2
God Speaks Love Language #1: Words of Affirmation

1. Jeremiah 31:3 (NASB).
2. John 13:1 (NASB).
3. 2 Timothy 3:16-17; 2 Peter 1:20-21.
4. Genesis 1:26-27.
5. Hebrews 2:7; cf. Psalm 8:5.
6. Isaiah 48:17-18.
7. Isaiah 41:10; Jeremiah 29:11; 31:3,13.
8. John 5:24; 6:35, 40; 10:27-30; Revelation 22:12-13, 17.
9. Luke 23:34.
10. John 10:9-11.
11. Charles Dudley Warner, ed., vol. 23, *Library of the World's Best Literature* (New York: J. A. Hill & Co., 1896), 9334, 9340.
12. Psalm 119:103-105, 111, 114, 162-165.
13. Psalms 40:16; 69:30-31; 119:97-98; 145:21; 146:1-2.
14. Psalm 119:89, 91-93.

Chapter 3
God Speaks Love Language #2: Quality Time

1. See Genesis 1-3.
2. Genesis 18:17.
3. Psalm 145:17-18.
4. Isaiah 43:1-2.
5. Psalm 116:1-2.
6. James 4:8.
7. See John 14:23-26.
8. John 17:24; *see also* 14:16-18.
9. Mark 3:14.
10. George Muller, *Autobiography of George Muller, the Life of Trust* (Grand Rapids: Baker, 1981), 115.
11. Ibid., 89, 101, 108-9.
12. Ibid., 82.
13. Ibid., 138-39.
14. Ibid., 206-7.

15. Ibid., 62.

16. Ibid., 206.

17. *See* Jonathan Edwards, *The Life and Diary of David Brainerd* (Grand Rapids: Baker, 1989); E. M. Bounds, *Power Through Prayer* (Minneapolis: World Wide Publications, 1989); Charles G. Finney, *The Autobiography of Charles G. Finney* (Minneapolis: Bethany Fellowship, 1977); and Basil Miller, *Praying Hyde: A Man of Prayer* (Grand Rapids: Zondervan, 1943).

18. C. Austin Miles, "In the Garden," verses 1-2 and refrain. In public domain.

CHAPTER 4
God Speaks Love Language #3: Gifts

1. R. G. LeTourneau, *Mover of Men and Mountains* (Chicago: Moody, 1972), 143.

2. Ibid., 263.

3. Ibid., 79.

4. Ibid., 204.

5. Ibid., 205.

6. Adapted from LeTourneau, *Mover of Men and Mountains,* 105.

7. LeTourneau, *Mover of Men and Mountains,* 278.

8. Ibid., 33.

9. Ibid., 274.

10. Ibid., 280.

11. Genesis 1:27, 29-31; emphasis added.

12. Revelation 22:12-14, 16-17.

13. Deuteronomy 7:13.

14. Deuteronomy 11:13-15.

15. 1 Kings 3:7, 9, 11-13.

16. John 3:17, 35-36.

17. John 16:16, 20.

18. John 16:23-24.

19. Ephesians 5:1-2.

20. James 1:17; 1 John 3:1-2.

21. Ephesians 4:11-12.

22. 1 Corinthians 12:7.

23. Matthew 25:34-40.

24. Psalm 19:1-3.

25. Matthew 7:7-11.

26. James 4:3.

CHAPTER 5
God Speaks Love Language #4: Acts of Service

1. José Luis Gonzalez-Balado, *Mother Teresa: In My Own Words* (Liguori, Mo.: Liguori, 1996), ix.

2. Ibid., x.

3. Ibid., 24, 26, 30.

4. Ibid., 34.

5. Ibid., 33.

6. Ibid., 38, 80.

7. Ibid., 107.

8. Ibid., 108-9.

9. Romans 15:6; see also 2 Corinthians 1:3 and Ephesians 1:3.

10. Psalm 115:4-7, 9, 12-13.

11. Luke 4:18-19 (Jesus' quotation of Isaiah 61:1-2).

12. Luke 4:21, 24.

13. John 17:1-5.

14. John 14:1-7.

15. John 14:8-11.

16. John 15:24-25.

17. Jesus brought back to life a widow's son (Luke 7:11-17), a ruler's daughter (Luke 8:41-42, 49-56), and a male friend who had been in the grave four days (John 11:1-44).

18. John 15:9.

19. John 15:12-13; Luke 23:34.

20. Romans 5:6-8.

21. John 17:24, 26.

22. C. S. Lewis, *Mere Christianity* (New York: Macmillan, 1960), 55-56.

CHAPTER 6
God Speaks Love Language #5: Physical Touch

1. Psalms 68:5; 27:10.

2. Genesis 32:25, 30.

3. Exodus 34:29, 33.

4. Mark 10:13.

5. Mark 10:15-16.

6. John 9:11.

7. Matthew 9:27, 29-30.

8. Matthew 8:2-3, 15.

9. Matthew 17:2-3, 5-8; see also Mark 9:2-10 and Luke 9:28-36.

10. John 13:1-4.

11. John 13:12-15, 17.

12. José Luis Gonzalez-Balado, *Mother Teresa: In My Own Words* (Liguori, Mo.: Liguori, 1996), 35.

13. Acts 3:6-10.

14. Acts 3:12-13, 16.

15. Acts 3:18-21.

16. Acts 9:4-9.

17. Acts 9:17-19.

18. Acts 9:20-22.

CHAPTER 8
Learning to Speak New Dialects of Love

1. See, for example, Romans 1:21.

2. Robert J. Morgan, *From This Verse* (Nashville: Nelson, 1998), 362.

3. Psalm 42:1-2.

4. Matthew 10:42.

5. Acts 10:38.

6. John 20:30-31.

7. Luke 7:38.

CHAPTER 9
Love Languages and God's Discipline

1. For further information on the relationship between love languages and discipline, see Ross Campbell and Gary Chapman, *The Five Love Languages of Children* (Chicago: Northfield, 1997), 117, 124-27.

2. Hebrews 12:5-7, 10-11.

3. John 10:11, 17-18.

4. John 11:25.

5. John 20:30-31.

6. Psalm 42:1-2.

7. C. S. Lewis, *The Problem of Pain* (New York: HarperCollins, 2001), 91.

8. 2 Corinthians 11:22–12:10.

9. 2 Timothy 4:6-7.

CHAPTER 10
Whatever the Language, Let Love Prevail

1. Jeremiah 29:11-13.

2. Michael Cassidy, "Loose in the South African Fire," C. S. Lewis Foundation Summer Institute (Oxbridge '98), 24 July 1998; author's personal notes.

3. Heidi Soderstrom, "Prescription: Hope," *The Commission,* May 1999, 34-37.

4. 1 John 4:20 (author paraphrase).

5. Matthew 5:43-47.

6. John 8:42-47.

7. Philippians 2:4; Romans 12:10.

8. Romans 5:7-8.

9. Romans 5:5.

10. John 19:30.

11. Matthew 27:51-54.

12. Revelation 13:8.

13. John 13:34-35.

14. David Wilkerson with John and Elizabeth Sherrill, *The Cross and the Switchblade* (New York: Random House, 1963), 72.

15. See Psalm 68:6; Romans 12:5; Ephesians 3:15.

16. Ephesians 3:14-21.

17. John 13:34-35.

EPILOGUE
The God Who Speaks Your Language

1. Jeremiah 29:13.

2. Matthew 11:28-30.

3. John 10:27-28.

4. James 4:8.

5. Matthew 20:28; Acts 10:38.

6. 1 John 1:1; John 1:14.

7. John 14:23-24.

8. John 14:26.

9. John 20:31; see also John 21:25.

10. 1 John 4:19-21.

11. Matthew 22:36-40.

12. 1 John 4:7-10.

13. Acts 17:24-31.

14. Frederick M. Lehman, "The Love of God." In public domain.

15. John 23:34.

16. See Colossians 1:21-22.

17. See John 3:16-18; 1 John 1:9.

18. John 10:11.

19. 1 John 4:8, 16.

GUIDE *for*

GROUP STUDY

The following suggestions are to help facilitate a group discussion of each chapter's content. Group members should always be encouraged to share answers, but never forced to.

CHAPTER 1/UNDERSTANDING THE FIVE LOVE LANGUAGES

(1) Share stories with other group members about times when you encountered language difficulties or problems communicating with someone else. Describe the situation and the feelings experienced. (Was the lack of communication comic? Sad? Dangerous? Worth the effort?)

Then discuss the opposite extreme—a time when you and another person were really connecting with one another. How does it feel to realize someone fully understands not only your words, but also the thoughts and feelings behind them?

(2) Discuss: *What do you suspect is your primary love language: words of affirmation, quality time, gifts, acts of service, or physical touch? On a scale of 1 (least) to 10 (most), how certain are you?* If group members know each other fairly well, let them provide input for one another at this point to verify or challenge a person's response. Explain that later chapters will provide much additional information to confirm or possibly change these early opinions.

(3) Have a volunteer read 1 Corinthians 13—the "love chapter" of the Bible. The passage should be familiar to most group members. But as they hear it this time, have them listen in terms of their designated love languages. For example, how would this classic description of love pertain to words of affirmation, the giving of gifts, physical touch, and so forth?

(4) Ask members to share any questions they have at this early stage, and have a volunteer record their responses. As you go through the rest of the book, look for sections that address the questions on your list.

(5) You might also consider how each participant might use his or her love language for the benefit of the group in future meetings. For example, someone who prefers words of affirmation might be more willing to pray; those who speak the language of gifts might prepare (or at least organize) refreshments; those who respond to quality time might host the meetings and encourage members to stay afterward for a while; etc.

CHAPTER 2/GOD SPEAKS LOVE LANGUAGE #1: WORDS OF AFFIRMATION

(1) Begin by having group members describe a time when someone's

words meant a great deal to them. It might be helpful to have each person think of at least two examples: once long ago that had a lasting effect on their lives, and another that has occurred just recently.

(2) Have group members share some of their favorite promises from the Bible. If they are slow getting started, have volunteers look up and read these that were included in the chapter:

Psalm 119:103-105	**Psalm 119:111**	**Psalm 119:114**	**Psalm 119:162-165**
Isaiah 41:10	**Jeremiah 29:11**	**Jeremiah 31:3**	**Jeremiah 31:13**
John 5:24	**John 6:35**	**John 6:40**	**John 10:27-30**
Revelation 22:12-13	**Revelation 22:17**		

Discuss: *Some people would consider these verses "just words." What is it about them that provides the sense of affirmation for you?*

(3) Give group members the opportunity to practice this love language among one another as you verbally affirm each person present. If you are still relative strangers, you might not be ready to do so. But if you know one another, begin with one person and let others affirm what it is about that person that they appreciate. Then move to the next person and on around the group. When finished, discuss how it felt to have so much focused attention and affirmation.

(4) Close with a sentence prayer, giving everyone the opportunity to express short statements of affirmation to God. (See King David's examples on page 44).

NOTE: In preparation for the next meeting, you might want to ask volunteers to do a little research on the four people mentioned toward the end of Chapter 3: David Brainard, E. M. Bounds, Charles Finney, and Praying John Hyde. These will be unfamiliar names to many people, yet their examples of quality time with God have inspired countless others.

CHAPTER 3/GOD SPEAKS LOVE LANGUAGE #2: QUALITY TIME

(1) Discuss: *Why did you decide to participate in this group?* After each person responds, see how many expressed, in one form or another, the desire to spend quality time with others. Some were most likely drawn by the topic, but others may have been equally attracted to the format. For example, someone may respond that he or she was personally invited by another member, yet may not consciously realize that accepting the invitation was for the opportunity of spending quality time with that person.

(2) If you opted to have volunteers research David Brainard, E. M. Bounds, Charles Finney, and Praying John Hyde, have them give their reports at this point. Be sure to include how spending quality time with God affected the life and ministry of each person. If you didn't choose to do so, spend time discussing the life of George Mueller described in the chapter: *What did you think of his devotion to prayer and quality time with God? Do you think his commitment to God and his work with the orphanages were interrelated? Why or why not?*

(3) Ask: *What people do you know personally who appear to demonstrate quality time as a primary love language? How does it affect their relationship with God? How does it influence their relationships with other people?*

(4) Have volunteers look up the following passages (all mentioned in the chapter) and discuss what you might learn and apply from each one about quality time with God:

- Abraham and God (Genesis 18)
- Jesus and His disciples (Mark 4:30-41)
- Jesus, Mary, and Martha (Luke 10:38-42)

(5) Close by spending a little quality time with God as a group. Let all who are willing express themselves to God in a way that is comfortable for them. (Although the focus is on quality time, those with the gift of touch might give hugs to other members, those with words of affirmation might pray or sing, and so forth.)

CHAPTER 4/GOD SPEAKS LOVE LANGUAGE #3: GIFTS

(1) Discuss: *Who is someone whose generosity and gift-giving you admire and would go out of your way to meet, given the opportunity?*

(2) Explain that people have different opinions about how much to expect from God, and let members describe their personal beliefs about God as a giver. For example:

- *Are success and wealth proof of God's blessing?*
- *Does God give to each person equally? (If not, why not?)*
- *If we don't use the gifts God gives us, are we in danger of losing them?*

After participants express their opinions, discuss the concept of God's gifts as a love language. While people may disagree on some aspects of His gifts, few can argue that God gives to people out of love, and is pleased when they then give to one another.

(3) Spend a little time discussing spiritual gifts. First have a volunteer read 1 Corinthians 12:4-7 and point out, as was noted in chapter 4, that every believer in Christ has been given distinct abilities to perform certain tasks in the church. Lists of spiritual gifts are found in Romans 12:6-8; 1 Corinthians 12:8-10, 28-30; and Ephesians 4:11-13.

If this is a new topic for group members, you may want to provide additional resources (or save the discussion until there is more time available). But if they are familiar with spiritual gifts, let them share what they believe their gifts are and how they use each gift for the good of the church. And if they know one another well, encourage them to identify perceived spiritual gifts in one another.

(4) Have volunteers read Luke 21:1-2 and Matthew 10:42. Explain that two pennies or a cup of cold water may seem like insignificant gifts, yet all heartfelt gifts are noticed (and rewarded) by Jesus. Then discuss other gifts that may seem small, yet could meet very real needs in your church and community. Perhaps your discussion will lead to suggestions for your group members to give to an established charitable organization where their gifts will express God's love to others in their immediate vicinity. If they tend to think of projects they might do to help others as a group, you might postpone the discussion until the next chapter and undertake it as an act of service.

CHAPTER 5/GOD SPEAKS LOVE LANGUAGE #4: ACTS OF SERVICE

(1) Have each person share a time (or times) when someone performed an act of service for him or her that had a dramatic and lasting effect.

(2) Encourage participants to describe acts of service they have done for other people. Try to get a variety of examples: seemingly small actions that had much larger results than expected, times when much effort went into an act of service with very little response from the recipient, acts that were anonymous or went completely unnoticed, etc. Discuss: *Even though our acts of service get different results, do you think God evaluates us based on those results?* Explain that God is pleased when His people show genuine love for others through service, regardless of how the recipients respond.

(3) Have a volunteer read Exodus 17:8-13. Discuss:
- *Which of the participants named do you think was primarily responsible for the Israelites' victory over the Amalekites?* (Moses was certainly a key figure. Joshua was leading the army. Yet Aaron and Hur were equally essential, despite the seemingly insignificant roles they played.)
- *Which of the characters do you most relate to? Why?*
- *Do you think most people give equal credit to the Aarons and Hurs who are willing to perform mundane service, or do they show more respect to those like Moses and Joshua? Why? Do you think those in the church do any better than the general population at recognizing everyone's contributions?*

(4) It can be a little intimidating to cite Mother Teresa as a model for acts of service. Yet she became known throughout the world for seeing a need that no one else was addressing and working consistently to meet that need as an act of service to God. Can your group members identify similarly neglected needs in your church? Neighborhood? City? Are there things your group members would be willing to do as acts of service to meet some of the needs they identify?

CHAPTER 6/GOD SPEAKS LOVE LANGUAGE #5: PHYSICAL TOUCH

(1) Ask group members to determine how comfortable they are with physical touch in each of the following settings. Have them respond with a rating from 1 (least comfortable) to 10 (most comfortable).

- Kisses, hugs, and such among immediate family members
- A hug from a casual acquaintance of the same gender in a public place
- A hug from a casual acquaintance of the opposite gender in a public place
- Holding hands of strangers while singing in church
- The unexpected hand of a homeless person on their shoulder at a city park
- The embrace of an elderly person while visiting a nursing facility

As participants respond, encourage them to be honest and nonjudgmental of others because there are numerous valid reasons why someone may not be comfortable with physical touch. And they are likely to discover a variance in tolerance levels of physical touch.

(2) Discuss: *What examples can you recall from the chapter of physical touch in the ministry of Jesus? Why do you think the Bible says so much about Jesus' propensity to touch others?* (He gladly held little children, washed His disciples' feet, touched lepers and others while healing them, etc. He taught much about love, but physical touch was one tangible way to not only make that kind of love more real for those He met, but also as a model for others to follow.)

(3) Have a volunteer read Luke 8:40-48. Discuss:

- *Why do you think this woman was so compelled to touch Jesus?*

- *In the midst of a pressing crowd, how did Jesus know one particular individual had intentionally touched Him?*
- *What made the touch of the woman different from that of all the other people who were touching Jesus?*
- *Jesus was on His way to see a very sick girl (who would be dead by the time He arrived). What do we learn about Him from His willingness to stop and seek out one particular person before moving on?*

(4) Have volunteers share times in their lives when they felt most like God was touching them. Then ask them to think of ways that they might attempt to "touch" God. Without the physical presence of Jesus, how might that be possible? (When Jesus returned to the Father, He promised to send a replacement. Believers have access to God and can feel His presence through His Holy Spirit. The Spirit also intercedes for believers by "translating" their innermost feelings and presenting them to God the Father [Romans 8:26-27]. In that sense, God is always within reach.)

(5) Close with some kind of physical touch that is comfortable for everyone present (holding hands to pray, hugging one another, etc.). As you do, thank God as a group for this love language (and all the previous ones as well).

CHAPTER 7/DISCOVERING YOUR PRIMARY LOVE LANGUAGE

(1) Ask group members to recall what they cited as their primary love language during the first meeting (chapter 1). Discuss:
- *Has anyone come to a different conclusion during the past several sessions? If so, has that made a difference in how you relate to other people or God?*

(2) Have a volunteer read 1 Samuel 17:4-11, 32-40. The David vs. Goliath story will probably be familiar to most, so focus on David's choice of attire. Discuss:

- *Do you think David was naïve or unaware of the severity of the challenge before him?* (If not, why did he agree to fight when no one else would?)
- *What practical steps did King Saul take to protect David?*
- *Why did David decline Saul's offer?*
- *What was the ultimate result?* (See 1 Samuel 17:41-54 if necessary.)
- *How might this story relate to love languages?*

Point out that it would have made perfect sense for most people to wear all the protective gear possible before facing such an opponent. David was willing to give it a try, but it wasn't right for him. Similarly, one person's love language may appear to be the right approach, but other people have different (and equally valid) alternatives.

(3) Have your group members spend the bulk of their time discussing the three questions provided in the chapter, first in regard to one another, and then in regard to God.

- *How do I most often express love to other people (or God)?*
- *What do I complain about most often?*
- *What do I request most often?*

(4) Ask group members to explain how an increased awareness of their love languages has affected the two areas mentioned in the chapter: (1) Their level of self-understanding; and (2) Their ability to understand and help fellow believers. Encourage a variety of stories as examples.

(5) Close with a prayer, thanking God for any positive improvements so far and asking Him to let those changes be just the beginning of an ongoing closer bond with Him and with other people.

CHAPTER 8/LEARNING TO SPEAK NEW DIALECTS OF LOVE

(1) Have group members describe a time or times when they found themselves in a situation where they were completely out of their element (meeting new in-laws, work situations, attending new churches, vacationing, etc.). What made them feel out of place? How did they respond? Did they learn anything positive from the experience?

(2) Have a volunteer read Luke 10:1-12, 16-17. Explain that the passage describes an assignment Jesus gave to a group of His followers. Most (if not all) would have been familiar and comfortable with the Jewish rites and rituals, so their mission was a rather challenging one. Discuss:

- *How would you like to have been among this group? Why? How do you think you would have handled the assignment?*
- *What would have been your hopes? Your fears? Your biggest challenge?*
- *How well would you have handled living with strangers? How would you have responded to being rejected?*
- *How do you think your final response would compare to that of the disciples* (v. 17)?

(3) Summarize: *This was a lengthy chapter with a number of specific ideas involving all five love languages.* Ask: *Did any of the suggestions sound intriguing to you?* Let participants answer and explain why.

(4) Discuss: *After we discover our primary love language, why does*

it matter whether or not we "speak" other languages as well, or add different "dialects"? Someone should recall the chapter's challenge to keep worship from becoming ritual. What starts out as authentic can become mundane if we aren't careful. Perhaps group members could provide specific examples from their own experience.

(5) Challenge each person to experiment this week by attempting to use: (1) A love language other than their primary one; and (2) A different dialect of their own love language. For example, if they tend to worship privately, they might attempt more corporate worship this week. They might vary a time or location. They might move from religious to secular settings, or vice versa. Be sure to give them permission to fail. (Many people tend to avoid attempting new things due to fear of failure.)

Close with prayer, asking God to direct each person to new and different opportunities to speak languages of love this week. And be sure to schedule time at the next meeting for their reports.

CHAPTER 9/LOVE LANGUAGES AND GOD'S DISCIPLINE

(1) Follow up with the challenge from last week. Did anyone experiment with a new love language, or a different dialect of his or her primary love language? If so, what were the results?

(2) Ask group members to describe the type of discipline their parents enforced as they were growing up. (Answers should be in generalities. Try to avoid potentially embarrassing or painful details.) When everyone has responded who wishes to, explain that many times a person's initial image of God is formed by that of his or her parents. If the parents are strict and authoritarian, the person may assume a "heavenly

Father" to be the same. If parents are very laid back, the person might come to believe God isn't particularly interested in him or her. Ask: *For you, was "discipline" a positive, negative, or neutral word?*

(3) Discuss the positive aspects of discipline. Begin with self-discipline. Does anyone commit to an exercise regimen? A diet? Continuing education? Regular devotions? If so, have the person contrast the challenging aspects of discipline with the results.

Then broaden the topic to include discipline imposed by others. Can anyone recall an instance of being disciplined by a parent, teacher, employer, etc., that resulted in a significant turnaround of their attitudes or behavior? Or does someone have a story of raising children when a seemingly harsh discipline had a positive effect over time? Can you detect any connections between the effectiveness of the discipline and the person's love language?

(4) Have a volunteer read Hebrews 12:4-13 (much of which was quoted in Chapter 9). Discuss:
- *What is the author referring to when he uses the word "discipline"?* (v. 7)
- *What is the purpose of God's discipline?* (See also Romans 5:3-5.)
- *What is the motivation behind God's discipline?* (Hebrews 12:6, 10)
- *What are the desired results of God's discipline?* (v. 11)

Emphasize that while God's discipline is compared to that of a parent of a child, the difference is that God never has a bad day, gets frustrated, becomes too busy, or fails to empathize with how the one being disciplined will feel.

Have another volunteer read the Parable of the Prodigal Son (Luke 15:11-32) as others pay close attention to the actions and responses of the father. Stress that God's discipline should never be discussed or evaluated apart from His great love and forgiveness as illustrated in this parable.

(5) Discipline can be a difficult and sensitive issue. Close with a time for group members to reflect on their feelings about God's discipline, to ask opinions of other participants about their own methods of discipline, and share prayer requests for ongoing disciplinary problems in their lives and relationships. During this time, make it clear that understanding how the effectiveness of discipline pertains to a person's love language is not a license to attempt to manipulate others. Such knowledge should always be applied with much love, integrity, and genuine concern for the other person. The emphasis on love will be the theme of the next session.

CHAPTER 10/WHATEVER THE LANGUAGE, LET LOVE PREVAIL (AND EPILOGUE)

(1) Ask volunteers to recount a time in their lives when "love prevailed." (Accounts may include unusual friendships, times when love changed their plans, motivation to take a strong stand against a wrong, etc.) After several stories have been shared, consider to what extent the five love languages may have been involved (words of affirmation, quality time, gifts, acts of service, or physical touch). Also discuss to what extent those loving moments reflected the love of God.

(2) Discuss:

* *Have you ever encountered a so-called "lover of God" who didn't*

display genuine love? What was the situation? What was your response to the person?

- *How do you respond to the thought that God's love is unconditional? How does that consideration influence your daily life?*
- *How do you respond to the thought that God's love is everlasting? How does that consideration influence your daily life?*

(3) Have a volunteer read 1 John 4:7-21. Discuss:

- *Is anything in this passage new to you, or do you see any of these truths in a new light after completing this book?*
- *How important is love in your relationship with God? With other people?*
- *What do you think John meant when he wrote, "God is love"* (v. 16)?
- *What do you think he meant by, "Love is made complete among us"* (v. 17)?
- *How is love supposed to connect our worship to our daily lives?* (vv. 20-21)

(4) If you recall (or if you kept) the questions your participants had at the end of the first session, restate them here and see if they have been answered. If not, work as a group to determine the best way to find the answers.

(5) Save time for a review of the book as a whole. In this final review, be sure to include: (1) *How does God speak your primary love language;* and (2) *How do you reflect that love to others?*

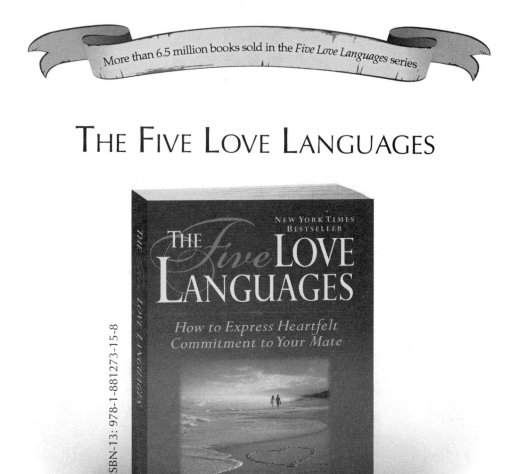

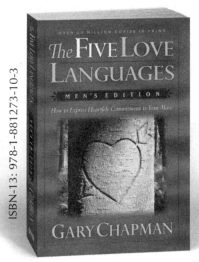
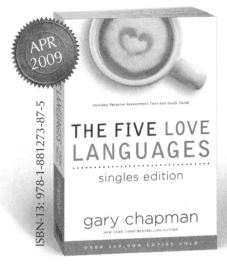

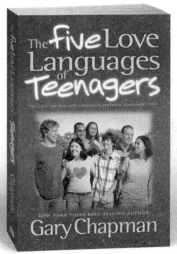
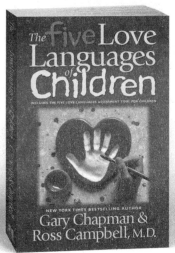

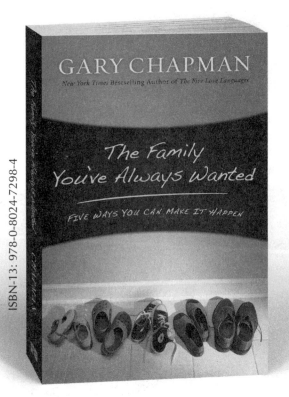

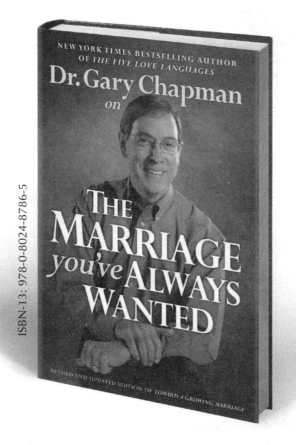

THE FIVE LANGUAGES OF APOLOGY

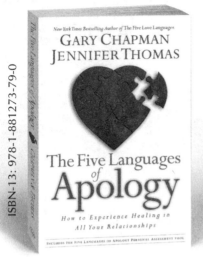

ISBN-13: 978-1-881273-79-0

Just as you have a distinct love language, you also hear and express the words and gestures of apology in a different language. This groundbreaking study of the way we apologize reveals that it's not a matter of will—it's a matter of how. By helping you identify the languages of apology, this book clears the way toward healing and sustaining vital relationships.

WWW.FIVELOVELANGUAGES.COM

ANGER

ISBN-13: 978-1-881273-88-2

We live in an angry society.

You can't escape it.

But this candid look at a volatile human emotion can help you deal with it productively.

WWW.FIVELOVELANGUAGES.COM

NORTHFIELD
PUBLISHING

1-800-678-8812 • MOODYPUBLISHERS.COM